hands-on
social
studies

Grade 4

REVISED EDITION

Jennifer Lawson

Karen Boyd

Barb Thomson

Linda McDowell

PORTAGE & MAIN PRESS

Winnipeg • Manitoba • Canada

Portage & Main Press acknowledges the financial support of the Government of Canada through the Book Publishing Industry Development Program (BPIDP) for our publishing activities.

**Library and Archives Canada
Cataloguing in Publication**

Lawson, Jennifer E. (Jennifer Elizabeth), 1959-
   Hands-on social studies : grade 4 /
   Jennifer Lawson. – Ontario ed.

Previous eds. written by Jennifer Lawson...
[et al.].
Includes bibliographical references.
ISBN 13: 978-1-55379-069-3

1. Social sciences – Study and teaching
(Elementary). 2.Social
sciences – Problems, exercises, etc. I.Title.

LB1530.L395 2005 372.83'044 C2005-905001-2

Series Editor: Leigh Hambly
Assistant Editor: Catherine Gerbasi
Book and Cover Design: Relish Design Ltd.
Illustrations: Meghan Eldridge, Jess Dixon

PORTAGE & MAIN PRESS

100-318 McDermot Avenue
Winnipeg, Manitoba, Canada R3A 0A2

E-mail: books@portageandmainpress.com
Tel: 204-987-3500
Toll Free: 1-800-667-9673
Fax: 1-866-734-8477

Contents

Introduction to *Hands-On Social Studies*

Program Introduction

The *Hands-On Social Studies* program focuses on developing students' knowledge, skills, and attitudes through active inquiry, problem solving, and decision making. Throughout all activities, students are encouraged to explore, investigate, and ask questions in order to heighten their own curiosity about and understanding of the world around them.

What Is Social Studies?

Social studies is an interdisciplinary study that draws from such traditional disciplines as history, geography, political studies, and economics. It involves the examination of communities, both locally and globally. In essence, social studies helps students learn about the world around them.

Social studies also involves the development of concepts as well as skills of inquiry and communication. Students apply these skills to develop an understanding of their world and to enable them to make decisions and solve problems in everyday life.

The Goals of Social Studies

The *Hands-On Social Studies* program has been designed to focus on the goals of the Social Studies Curriculum as identified by the Ontario Ministry of Education and Training (2004, revised). These goals are:

1. To understand the basic concepts of social studies, history, and geography.

2. To develop the skills, strategies, and habits of mind required for effective inquiry and communication, and for the application of the basic concepts of social studies, history, and geography to a variety of learning tasks.

3. To relate and apply the knowledge acquired through social studies and the study of history and geography to the world outside the classroom.

▶

Hands-On Social Studies Expectations

Heritage and Citizenship
Unit 1: Medieval Times

Overall Expectations

☐ Identify and describe major features of daily life and social organization in medieval European societies from about 500 to 1500 C.E. (Common Era).

☐ Use a variety of resources and tools to investigate the major events and influences of the era and determine how they shaped medieval society.

☐ Relate significant elements of medieval societies to comparable aspects of contemporary Canadian communities.

Specific Expectations

Knowledge and Understanding

☐ Describe the hierarchical structure of medieval society and the types of people in it, and explain how and why different groups cooperated or came into conflict at different times.

☐ Describe aspects of daily life for men, women, and children in medieval societies.

☐ Describe characteristics of castles and aspects of castle life.

☐ Outline the reasons for and some of the effects of medieval Europe's expanding contact with other parts of the world.

☐ Describe some of the ways in which religions shaped medieval society.

☐ Describe medieval agricultural methods and innovations, and explain why the innovations were important.

☐ Outline important ways in which medieval society changed over time, and give reasons for the changes.

Inquiry/Research and Communication Skills

☐ Formulate questions to guide research.

☐ Use primary and secondary sources to locate information about medieval civilizations.

☐ Use graphic organizers to summarize information.

☐ Draw and label maps or create models to illustrate features of medieval landscapes.

☐ Read and interpret maps relevant to the period.

☐ Use media works, oral presentations, written notes and descriptions, and drawings to communicate information about life in medieval society.

☐ Use appropriate vocabulary to describe their inquiries and observations.

Application

☐ Compare aspects of life in a medieval community and their own community.

☐ Make connections between social or environmental concerns of medieval times and similar concerns today.

☐ Use artistic expression to re-create or respond to imaginative works from medieval times.

Canada and World Connections
Unit 2: Canada's Provinces, Territories, and Regions

Overall Expectations

☐ Name and locate the various physical regions, provinces, and territories of Canada and identify the chief natural resources of each.

☐ Use a variety of resources and tools to determine the influence of physical factors on the economies and cultures of Ontario and the other provinces and territories.

☐ Identify, analyse, and describe economic and cultural relationships that link communities and regions within Ontario and across Canada.

▶

Specific Expectations

Knowledge and Understanding

☐ Explain the concept of a region.

☐ Identify the physical regions of Ontario and describe their characteristics.

☐ Explain how the St. Lawrence River and the Great Lakes systems shape or influence the human activity of their surrounding area.

☐ Identify Ontario's major natural resources and their uses and management.

☐ Identify and describe types of communities in each physical region of Ontario.

☐ Describe a variety of exchanges that occur among the communities and regions of Ontario and among the provinces and territories.

☐ Identify Canada's provinces and territories and its main physical regions.

☐ Describe and compare the environments of the physical regions of Canada.

☐ Identify the natural resources necessary to create Canadian products, and the provinces and territories from which they originate.

☐ Relate the physical environment to economic and cultural activities in the various provinces and territories.

Inquiry/Research and Communication Skills

☐ Formulate questions to guide research and clarify information on study topics.

☐ Use primary and secondary sources to locate information about natural resources and their uses.

☐ Use graphic organizers and graphs to sort information, clarify issues, solve problems, and make decisions.

☐ Use media works, oral presentations, written notes and descriptions, drawings, tables, and graphs to identify and communicate key information about the regions, provinces, and territories.

☐ Use appropriate vocabulary to describe their inquiries and observations.

Map, Globe, and Graphic Skills

☐ Locate on a map community boundaries and adjacent communities within a region.

☐ Locate on a map of Ontario and label the Great Lakes and other major bodies of water and waterways.

☐ Use a variety of sources to locate and label the physical regions of Canada on a map.

☐ Use cardinal and intermediate directions, pictorial and non-pictorial symbols, scale, and colour to locate and display geographic information on various maps.

☐ Use number and letter grids to locate places on base maps and road maps, and in atlases.

☐ Create and use a variety of thematic maps of Canada's physical features.

☐ Construct maps of transportation routes between local communities within a region.

☐ Construct maps of the provinces and territories, showing major roadways, railways, and cities, including capital cities.

☐ Prepare various forms of maps, using symbols and legends, to display places, transportation routes, and political boundaries in Canada.

Application

☐ Identify relationships, in a variety of fields, that link Ontario and the other provinces and territories.

☐ Compare two or more regions, with respect to their physical environments and exchanges of goods and services.

☐ Identify and describe a cause-and-effect relationship between the environment and the economy in a province or territory.

☐ Describe how technology affects the lives of people in an isolated community in Canada.

▶

Program Principles

1. Effective social studies programs involve hands-on inquiry, problem solving, and decision making.

2. The development of students' concepts, skills, and attitudes form the foundation of the social studies program.

3. Children have a natural curiosity about the world around them. This curiosity must be maintained, fostered, and enhanced through active learning.

4. Social studies activities must be meaningful, worthwhile, and connect to real-life experiences.

5. Children learn best by doing, rather than just by listening. The teacher, therefore, should focus on formulating and asking questions, rather than simply on telling. Teachers should also encourage students to ask questions. The teacher's major roles in the social studies program are to facilitate activities and to encourage thinking and reflection.

6. Social studies should be taught in correlation with other school subjects. Themes and topics of study should integrate ideas and skills from several core areas whenever possible.

7. The social studies program should encompass a wide range of educational resources, including nonfiction research material, audio-visual resources, technology, as well as people and places in the local community (such as museums).

8. Assessment of student learning in social studies should be designed to focus on performance and understanding, and should be conducted through meaningful assessment techniques carried on throughout the units of study.

Program Implementation

Program Resources

The *Hands-On Social Studies* program is arranged in activities or lessons – a format that makes it easy for teachers to plan and implement.

Units are the selected topics of study for the grade level. The units relate directly to the expectations identified on pages 2 and 3, which were set forth in the Ontario Social Studies Curriculum (2004, revised) document. Each unit is organized as follows:

Books for Children and Web Sites: The unit opens with a list of children's books and several annotated web sites that relate to the topic.

Introduction: This section introduces the topic of study. It provides a general outline for the unit, general background information for teachers, and relevant vocabulary words. Teachers will find a complete list of materials required for the unit, including equipment, visuals, and materials that can be found in the classroom and in the home.

Activities: The unit activities are organized into topics based on the specific expectations. Each topic includes:

Background Information for Teachers: Some activities provide teachers with content knowledge required to present the lesson. This information is offered in a clear, concise format and focuses specifically on the topic of study.

Materials: A complete list of materials required to conduct the main activity is given. The quantity of materials required will depend on how you conduct the activities. If students are working individually, you will need enough materials

▶

for each student. If students are working in groups, the materials required will be significantly reduced. Many of the items are for the teacher to use for display purposes, or to make charts for recording students' ideas. In some cases, visual materials (i.e., large pictures, maps, sample charts, and diagrams) have been included with the activity to assist the teacher in presenting ideas and questions and encouraging discussion.

Activity: Each activity includes a step-by-step procedure – such as higher-level questioning techniques and suggestions – that encourage discussion, inquiry, decision making, and problem solving.

Activity Sheet: Reproducible activity sheets are designed to correlate with the specific expectations of the activity. Many of these are used during the activity to record results of investigations. Others are used as a follow-up to the activities. Students may work independently or in small groups on these sheets, or you may choose to read through them together and complete them in a large-group setting. Activity sheets can also be made into overheads or large experience charts. Since it is also important for students to learn to construct their own charts and recording formats, teachers can use these activity sheets as examples of ways to record and communicate ideas about an activity. Students can then create their own sheets rather than use the ones provided.

Extension: Included are optional activities to extend, enrich, and reinforce the expectations.

Activity Centre: Some topics have independent student activities that focus on the expectations.

Assessment Suggestions: Throughout each unit, several suggestions are made for assessing student learning. Again, these assessment strategies focus specifically on the expectations of a particular activity topic. Assessment is dealt with in detail in the next section of the *Hands-On Social Studies* program. Keep in mind that the suggestions are merely ideas to consider – you may also refer to the other assessment strategies referred to in the next section, or use your own techniques.

Classroom Environment

The classroom setting is an important component of the learning process. An active environment – one that gently hums with the purposeful conversations and activities of students – indicates that meaningful learning is taking place. When studying a specific topic, the room should display related objects and materials, student work, pictures and posters, maps, graphs, and charts made during activities, and summary charts of important concepts taught and learned. These visuals reinforce concepts and skills that have been emphasized during social studies activities.

Planning Units (Time Lines)

Certainly, no two groups of students will cover topics and material at the same rate. Planning the duration of each unit is the responsibility of the teacher. In some cases, the activities described herein will not be completed during one block of time and will have to be carried over. In other cases, you may observe that the students are especially interested in one topic, and you may decide to expand upon it. The individual needs of your class should be considered – there are no strict time lines involved in the *Hands-On Social Studies* program. It is important, however, to spend enough time on every unit in the program so

▶

that students focus on all of the curriculum expectations established for their grade level.

Classroom Management

Although active learning is emphasized throughout this program, the manner in which these experiences are handled is up to you. In some instances, you may have all students working with materials and resources individually; in others, you may choose to use small-group settings. Small groups encourage the development of social skills, enable all students to be active in the learning process, and mean less cost in terms of material and equipment. Again, classroom management is up to you; it is the teacher who, ultimately, determines how the students in his or her care function best in the learning environment.

Social Studies Skills: Guidelines for Teachers

While involved in the *Hands-On Social Studies* program, students use a variety of skills while answering questions, solving problems, and making decisions. The following list provides some guidelines for teachers when encouraging students' skill development in certain areas.

Communication

In social studies, one communicates by means of visuals, maps, diagrams, graphs, charts, models, symbols, as well as written and spoken language. Communicating spatial and statistical information through visuals includes:

- examining and discussing visuals
- drawing pictures and labelled diagrams
- reading and interpreting a variety of maps
- making and labelling maps
- reading and interpreting data from tables and charts

- making tables and charts
- reading and interpreting data from graphs
- making graphs
- making models
- using oral and written language

Visuals

Students should be given many opportunities to examine and discuss visuals related to topics of study. Visuals include illustrations, artwork, photographs, and diagrams. Observation skills are developed by examining such visuals. In turn, students should be encouraged to draw pictures and labelled diagrams to communicate their understanding of concepts and ideas.

Mapping Skills

When presenting maps or when students make their own maps as part of a specific activity, there are guidelines that should be followed. Maps must always have an appropriate title that indicates the information being presented. On most maps, a compass rose is used to identify directions. Maps also include a legend, which describes the symbols used on the map. In addition, students should become familiar with the use of scale on maps to communicate relative area. Students should become proficient in reading maps, as well as in producing maps that include these components.

Maps convey various types of information – geographical locations, physical land features, population, natural resources, vegetation, and so on. Students should be provided with opportunities to use, read, and construct a variety of maps in order to develop these skills of communication in social studies.

Canada's Land Regions

Legend
- Appalachians
- Arctic Lowlands
- Canadian Shield
- Cordillera
- Great Lakes/St. Lawrence Lowlands/
- Hudson Bay Lowlands
- Interior Plains

0   500   1000 km

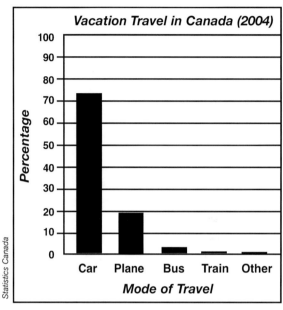

Vacation Travel in Canada (2004)

Percentage (vertical axis, 0 to 100)

Mode of Travel: Car, Plane, Bus, Train, Other

Statistics Canada

Graphs

There are guidelines that should be followed when presenting graphs, or when students are constructing them.

- A *bar graph* is a common form of communication. Bar graphs should always be titled so that the information communicated is easily understood. The title should be capitalized in the same manner as one would title a story.

  Both axes of the graph should also be titled and capitalized in the same way. In most cases, graduated markings are noted on one axis and the objects or events being compared are noted on the other. On a bar graph, the bars must be separate, as each bar represents a distinct piece of data.

- A *broken line graph* is used to communicate data when measuring an object or event over a period of time. For example, a broken line graph may be used to present local daily temperatures over a period of one week.

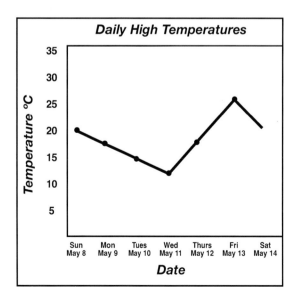

Daily High Temperatures

Temperature °C (vertical axis, 5 to 35)

Date: Sun May 8, Mon May 9, Tues May 10, Wed May 11, Thurs May 12, Fri May 13, Sat May 14

▶

- A *pie graph* is used to present information about one particular object or event. For example, a pie graph can be used to indicate energy consumption in Canada.

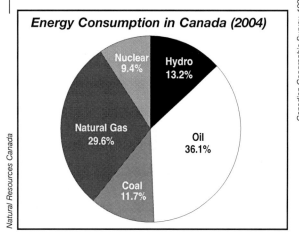

Energy Consumption in Canada (2004)

Nuclear 9.4%
Hydro 13.2%
Oil 36.1%
Coal 11.7%
Natural Gas 29.6%

Natural Resources Canada

Charts

Charts require appropriate titles, and both columns and rows need specific headings. Again, all of these titles and headings require capitalization. Charts can be made in the form of checklists or can include room for additional written information and data.

Location of Countries of the World

Country	Northern Hemisphere	Southern Hemisphere
Canada	✔	
Australia		✔
New Zealand		✔

Area of Provinces and Territories

Province/ Territory	Land (km²)	Freshwater (km²)	Total (km²)
Yukon	478970	4480	483450
Manitoba	548360	101590	649950
Ontario	891190	117390	1008580

Canadian Geographic Survey, 1998

Language

Communicating involves using the language and terminology of social studies. Communication can be complex – it often includes technical terms and words from many languages. Students should be encouraged to use the appropriate vocabulary related to the topics of study (e.g., *province, country, economy, resources, culture, feudal system*). Students should be encouraged to use the vocabulary and terminology in written form as well as orally. Consider developing whole-class or individual glossaries whereby students can record the terms learned, then define them in their own words. Glossaries can also include sketches, labelled diagrams, and examples.

Research

Research involves locating information from a variety of sources, organizing the information, and presenting information – either orally or in written form. For best results, teachers should always provide a structure for the research, indicating questions to be answered, as well as a format for conducting the research. Suggestions for research guidelines are presented regularly throughout the **Hands-On Social Studies** program.

Assessment Plan

The *Hands-On Social Studies* Assessment Plan

The *Hands-On Social Studies* program provides a variety of assessment tools that enable you to build a comprehensive and authentic daily assessment plan for your students. These assessment tools can be used to help teachers identify student achievement levels as outlined in the Ontario Social Studies Curriculum (2004, revised) document.

Embedded Assessment

Use the questions provided with each activity to assess students as they work. These questions promote higher-level thinking skills, active inquiry, problem solving, and decision making. Anecdotal record and observations are examples of embedded assessment.

- **Anecdotal Records:** Recording observation during social studies activities is critical in having an authentic view of a student's progress. The anecdotal record sheet presented on page 13 provides the teacher with a format for recording individual or group observations.

- **Individual Student Observations:** During activities when a teacher wishes to focus more on individual students, you may wish to use the individual student observation sheet on page 14. This black line master provides more space for comments and is especially useful during conferencing, interviews, or individual student presentations.

Data collected from anecdotal records and individual student observations can help teachers identify the achievement level of students according to their performance on given tasks.

Performance Assessment

Performance assessment is a planned, systematic observation and assessment based on students actually doing a specific social studies activity.

- **Rubrics:** To assess students' performances on a specific task, rubrics are used in the *Hands-On Social Studies* program to standardize and streamline scoring. A sample rubric and a black line master for teacher use are included on pages 15 and 16. For any specific activity, the teacher selects four criteria that relate directly to the expectations of students for the specific activity being assessed. To determine a rubric score for the assessment from a total of four marks, students are then given a check mark point for each criterion accomplished. These rubric scores can then be transferred to the rubric class record on page 17.

  The rubrics have been designed to complement the achievement levels, as a four point scale is used to identify student performance.

Cooperative Skills

In order to assess students' ability to work effectively in a group, teachers must observe the interaction within these groups. A cooperative skills teacher assessment sheet is included on page 18 for teachers to use while conducting such observations.

Student Self-Assessment

It is important to encourage students to reflect on their own learning in social studies. For this purpose, teachers will find a student self-assessment sheet (page 19), as well as a cooperative skills self-assessment sheet (page 20).

▶

Portfolios

With student input, select work to include in a social studies portfolio. This can include activity sheets, maps, graphs, research projects, photographs of projects, as well as other written material. Use the portfolio to reflect the student's progress in social studies over the course of the school year. Black line masters are included to organize the portfolio (social studies portfolio table of contents on page 21 and the social studies portfolio entry record on page 22).

Summative Achievement Levels

At the end of each unit, the teacher can determine achievement levels for each student. All assessment information gathered throughout the unit can be used to identify these levels, by referring to the chart on pages 11 and 12. A black line master is included on page 23 for recording this information.

Note: In each unit of the *Hands-On Social Studies* program, assessment suggestions are provided for several lessons. It is important to keep in mind that these are merely suggestions. Teachers are encouraged to use the assessment strategies in a wide variety of ways, build an effective assessment plan with these assessment ideas, and rely on their own valuable experiences as educators.

ACHIEVEMENT CHART FOR SOCIAL STUDIES, HISTORY, AND GEOGRAPHY

Category	Level 1	Level 2	Level 3	Level 4

Knowledge and Understanding Subject-specific content acquired in each grade (knowledge), and the comprehension of its meaning and significance (understanding)

The student:

Category	Level 1	Level 2	Level 3	Level 4
Knowledge of content (e.g., facts, terms, definitions)	- demonstrates limited knowledge of content	- demonstrates some knowledge of content	- demonstrates considerable knowledge of content	- demonstrates thorough knowledge of content
Understanding of content (e.g., concepts, ideas, theories, procedures, processes, methodologies, and/or technologies)	- demonstrates limited understanding of content	- demonstrates some understanding of content	- demonstrates considerable understanding of content	- demonstrates thorough understanding of content

Thinking The use of critical and creative thinking skills and/or processes

The student:

Category	Level 1	Level 2	Level 3	Level 4
Use of planning skills (e.g., focusing research, gathering information, organizing an inquiry, asking questions, setting goals)	- uses planning skills with limited effectiveness	- uses planning skills with some effectiveness	- uses planning skills with considerable effectiveness	- uses planning skills with a high degree of effectiveness
Use of processing skills (e.g., analysing, generating, integrating, synthesizing, evaluating, detecting point of view and bias)	- uses processing skills with limited effectiveness	- uses processing skills with some effectiveness	- uses processing skills with considerable effectiveness	- uses processing skills with a high degree of effectiveness
Use of critical/creative thinking processes (e.g., inquiry process, problem-solving process, decision- making process, research process)	- uses critical/creative thinking processes with limited effectiveness	- uses critical/creative thinking processes with some effectiveness	- uses critical/creative thinking processes with considerable effectiveness	- uses critical/creative thinking processes with a high degree of effectiveness

Communication The conveying of meaning through various forms

The student:

Category	Level 1	Level 2	Level 3	Level 4
Expression and organization of ideas and information (e.g., clear expression, logical organization) in oral, visual, and written forms	- expresses and organizes ideas and information with limited effectiveness	- expresses and organizes ideas and information with some effectiveness	- expresses and organizes ideas and information with considerable effectiveness	- expresses and organizes ideas and information with a high degree of effectiveness

Source from: *The Ontario Curriculum, Social Studies, Grades 1-6, Revised 2004.*

Category	Level 1	Level 2	Level 3	Level 4

Communication (cont.)

The student:

Category	Level 1	Level 2	Level 3	Level 4
Communication for different audiences (e.g., peers, adults) and purposes (e.g., to inform, to persuade) in oral, visual, and written forms	- communicates for different audiences and purposes with limited effectiveness	- communicates for different audiences and purposes with some effectiveness	- communicates for different audiences and purposes with considerable effectiveness	- communicates for different audiences and purposes with a high degree of effectiveness
Use of conventions (e.g., conventions of form, map conventions), vocabulary, and terminology of the discipline in oral, visual, and written forms	- uses conventions, vocabulary, and terminology of the discipline with limited effectiveness	- uses conventions, vocabulary, and terminology of the discipline with some effectiveness	- uses conventions, vocabulary, and terminology of the discipline with considerable effectiveness	- uses conventions, vocabulary, and terminology of the discipline with a high degree of effectiveness

Application The use of knowledge and skills to make connections within and between various contexts

The student:

Category	Level 1	Level 2	Level 3	Level 4
Application of knowledge and skills (e.g., concepts, procedures, processes, and/or technologies) in familiar contexts	- applies knowledge and skills in familiar contexts with limited effectiveness	- applies knowledge and skills in familiar contexts with some effectiveness	- applies knowledge and skills in familiar contexts with considerable effectiveness	- applies knowledge and skills in familiar contexts with a high degree of effectiveness
Transfer of knowledge and skills (e.g., concepts, procedures, methodologies, technologies) to new contexts	- transfers knowledge and skills to new contexts with limited effectiveness	- transfers knowledge and skills to new contexts with some effectiveness	- transfers knowledge and skills to new contexts with considerable effectiveness	- transfers knowledge and skills to new contexts with a high degree of effectiveness
Making connections within and between various contexts (e.g., past, present, and future; environmental; social; cultural; spatial; personal; multidisciplinary)	- makes connections within and between various contexts with limited effectiveness	- makes connections within and between various contexts with some effectiveness	- makes connections within and between various contexts with considerable effectiveness	- makes connections within and between various contexts with a high degree of effectiveness

Source from: *The Ontario Curriculum, Social Studies, Grades 1-6, Revised 2004.*

Date:_____

Anecdotal Record

Purpose of Observation: _____

Student/Group	Student/Group
Comments	**Comments**
Student/Group	**Student/Group**
Comments	**Comments**
Student/Group	**Student/Group**
Comments	**Comments**

Date:_____

Individual Student Observations

Purpose of Observation: _____

Student _____

Observations

Student _____

Observations

Student _____

Observations

Sample Rubric

Social Studies Activity: _Mapping Canada's Capital Cities_

Social Studies Unit: _Provinces and Territories_

Date: _January 28_

4 – Full Accomplishment
3 – Substantial Accomplishment
2 – Partial Accomplishment
1 – Little Accomplishment

Criteria

Student	Appropriate Title	Compass Rose	Accurately labelled Capitals	Accurate Legend	Rubric Score /4
Jesse	✓		✓	✓	3
Suon	✓	✓	✓	✓	4

SAMPLE

Rubric

Social Studies Activity: _____

Social Studies Unit: _____

Date: _____

4 – Full Accomplishment
3 – Substantial Accomplishment
2 – Partial Accomplishment
1 – Little Accomplishment

Student	Criteria				Rubric Score /4

Rubric Class Record

Student	Unit/Activity/Date										
	Rubric Scores /4										

Scores on Specific Tasks	Achievement Level
1	Level 1
2	Level 2
3	Level 3
4	Level 4

Cooperative Skills
Teacher Assessment

Date: _____

Task: _____

_____

Group Member	Cooperative Skills				
	Contributes ideas and questions	Respects and accepts contributions of others	Negotiates roles and responsibilities of each group member	Remains focused and encourages others to stay on task	Completes individual commitment to the group

Comments: _____

_____

_____

_____

_____

Date: _____ Name: _____

Student Self-Assessment

Reflecting on My Learning

1. Social Studies Topic: _____

2. Social Studies Activity: _____

   _____

3. What I learned: _____

   _____

   _____

4. Diagrams, Maps, or Pictures:

   ```
   ┌─────────────────────────────────────────────┐
   │                                               │
   │                                               │
   │                                               │
   │                                               │
   │                                               │
   │                                               │
   │                                               │
   └─────────────────────────────────────────────┘
   ```

5. I would like to learn more about: _____

   _____

   _____

6. I would like to improve in: _____

   _____

   _____

Date:_____   Name: _____

Cooperative Skills Self-Assessment

Students in my group:

_____   _____

_____   _____

Group Work – How Did I Do Today?

Group Work	How I Did (✔)		
	Very Good	**Satisfactory**	**Needs Improvement**
I shared ideas and contributed to discussion.			
I listened to others and respected their ideas.			
I asked questions.			
I encouraged others.			
I helped with the work.			
I stayed on task.			

I did very well in _____

_____

Next time I would like to improve in _____

_____

Date: _____ **Name:** _____

Social Studies Portfolio Table of Contents

Entry	Date	Selection
1.	_____	_____
2.	_____	_____
3.	_____	_____
4.	_____	_____
5.	_____	_____
6.	_____	_____
7.	_____	_____
8.	_____	_____
9.	_____	_____
10.	_____	_____
11.	_____	_____
12.	_____	_____
13.	_____	_____
14.	_____	_____
15.	_____	_____
16.	_____	_____
17.	_____	_____
18.	_____	_____
19.	_____	_____
20.	_____	_____

Date:_____   Name: _____

Social Studies Portfolio Entry Record

This work was chosen by _____

This work is _____

_____

_____

I chose this work because _____

_____

_____

_____

_____

_____

_____

_____

- ✂ - - - -

Date:_____   Name: _____

Social Studies Portfolio Entry Record

This work was chosen by _____

This work is _____

_____

_____

I chose this work because _____

_____

_____

_____

_____

_____

_____

Teacher: _____

Summative Achievement Levels

Student	Achievement Levels	
	Unit 1: _____	Unit 2: _____

Heritage and Citizenship
Unit 1: Medieval Times

Books for Children

Aliki. *A Medieval Feast.* New York: Thomas Y. Crowell, 1983.

Andersen, Hans Christian. *The Princess and the Pea*. Natick, MA: Picture Book Studio, 1987.

Clements, Gillian. *The Truth About Castles*. Minneapolis, MN: Carolrhoda, 1997.

Cox, Phil Roxbee. *What Were Castles For?* Usborne Starting Point History. London: Usborne, 1995.

Cushman, Karen. *Catherine, Called Birdy*. New York: HarperCollins, 1994.

_____. *Matilda Bone*. New York: Clarion Books, 2000.

Dussling, Jennifer. *Gargoyles, Monsters in Stone*. New York: Grosset & Dunlap, 1999.

Grimm, Jakob, and Wilhelm Grimm. *Rapunzel*. Mankato, MN: Creative Education, 1984.

Gross, Gwen (adapted). *Knights of the Round Table.* A Step-Up Classic. New York: Random House, 1985.

Hodges, Margaret (adapted). *Saint George and the Dragon*. Boston: Little, Brown, 1984.

Ingle, Annie (adapted). *Robin Hood.* A Step-Up Classic. New York: Random House, 1991.

Macdonald, Fiona. *Everyday Life in the Middle Ages*. London: Macdonald & Co., 1984.

_____. *How Would You Survive in the Middle Ages?* New York: Franklin Watts, 1995.

Osborne, Will, and Mary Pope. *Knights and Castles.* A Stepping Stone Book. New York: Random House, 2000.

Steele, Philip. *Castles*. New York: Kingfisher, 1995.

Taylor, Barbara. *World of Castles*. Owing Mills, MD: Ottenheimer, 2000.

Web Sites

- **www.castles-of-britain.com/castle32.htm**

  Examine the design and history of the ancient castles of England, Scotland, and Wales. The history of common surnames of British heritage, derived from jobs performed in and around castles and manors in medieval times, is also provided.

- **www.pitt.edu/~medart/index.html**

  Medieval Art and Architecture: archival images of cathedrals, churches, abbeys, and castles in France and England. Includes both exterior and interior views.

- **www.learner.org/exhibits/middleages/**

  Enter this exhibit on the Middle Ages for information on feudal life, homes, religion, clothing, health, and more. With links to related resources on the web.

- **www.image.ox.ac.uk/**

  Bodleian Library, Oxford University. Hundreds of images of illuminated manuscripts arranged by century and country of origin.

- **www.islamicity.com/education**

  "Guide to Education Center" offers pages on Islamic art and architecture, illuminated manuscripts, and Muslim scientists and thinkers from the Middle Ages.

- **www.dsc.discovery.com/anthology/momentsintime/blackdeath/blackdeath.html**

  Discovery Channel: an interactive history of the bubonic plague in Europe – with maps that show the path of the Black Death through Europe, live audio transcripts, and much more.

- **www.godecookery.com**

  This excellent site offers medieval recipes from authentic sources adapted for the 21st-century kitchen. Includes facts on food and feasting in the Middle Ages.

- **www.medievalrepro.com**

  Medieval Reproductions produces high quality, historically accurate reproductions of medieval arms, armour, and art work. The online catalogue provides an excellent visual resource of medieval armour, with information on how armour is made.

- **www.fleurdelis.com**

  Fleur-de-lis Designs: click on "Heraldry" for a history of heraldry and the parts of a coat of arms. Click on "Symbolism" for descriptions and historic meanings of the imagery and colour used on coats of arms and crests.

- **http://mw.mcmaster.ca/**

  Medieval Women: An Interactive Exploration, McMaster University: follow the story of fifteen-year-old Christine through 15th-century France. Enter the Scriptorium for the text, images, and music used within this site.

- **www.vmi.edu/english/audio/GP_Knight_Baragona.html**

  An audio version of Chaucer's "The Knight's Portrait." Read in Middle English, students can hear how English was spoken in medieval times and compare it with today's English language.

Introduction

Note: The medieval period is a long and complex time in history. The content in this unit has been *simplified* to fit the age level of students in grade 4 and to present a survey of some significant features and events of the period.

Long, long ago, the woods really were deep, dark, and dangerous; and castles were built to defend against invaders. Kings ruled over all, and serfs obeyed their lords. We refer to this period of time as medieval times or the Middle Ages.

In this unit, the medieval age will be explored through a variety of activities. Students will learn about the feudal system and the ways of life of the people in the different levels of society. They will also learn about the historical impact of the Magna Carta and the role of the Church in medieval life.

To effectively teach the lessons in this unit, many pictures are needed. Students will benefit from opportunities to observe, draw, and discuss pictures of the objects they are studying. There are many interesting photographs of medieval castles, monasteries, cathedrals, abbeys, and convents. Pictures of these buildings are available in calendars and books, and on many web sites on the Internet.

Students can also learn about life in medieval times by examining art that was created by artists who lived in this age (about 500–1500 C.E.). Art prints are available in the form of cards and calendars through the New York Metropolitan Museum of Art. Examples of these and of illuminated manuscripts can be found on the Internet as well. Many books about medieval times include prints on medieval art. Make these available to students throughout the unit.

Information for Teachers

The following books, by Karen Cushman, describe life for female characters in different levels of medieval society. These books are recommended for readers ages 12 and up, but could be acceptable for younger students if read aloud by the teacher.

- *Catherine, Called Birdy*

  Catherine, Called Birdy is about the daughter of a not-so-wealthy knight and describes the unglamorous side of life for a nobleman's daughter.

- *Matilda Bone*

  Matilda Bone is about a peasant girl who apprentices with a bone mender. The story describes the limited medical knowledge of the time.

It is recommended teachers read the following book, by Frances Temple, for their own reference.

- *The Ramsay Scallop*

  The Ramsay Scallop describes the lives of two young nobles, a man and a fourteen-year-old girl as they undertake a pilgrimage to Spain. The Crusades are mentioned, and readers are introduced to Muslim characters and a brief explanation of the Islamic faith. There are also descriptions of the unsanitary conditions of the times and the methods used to construct mighty cathedrals.

Two other recommended books are:

- Gross, Gwen (adapted). *Knights of the Round Table*

- Ingle, Annie (adapted). *Robin Hood*

Social Studies Vocabulary

Throughout this unit, teachers should use, and encourage students to use, vocabulary such as: *medieval, Magna Carta, dame, lord, knight, squire, page, serf, Crusades, peasant, royalty, nobles, Islam, Judaism, Christianity, Roman Catholic, clergy, merchant, trade guild, manor, monastery, mosque, pilgrimage,* and *chivalry.*

It will be beneficial to provide students with booklets suitable for glossaries (See lesson 1, activity sheet B). On an ongoing basis, review the meanings of new words, and encourage students to record these words in their glossary and to use them correctly in discussions.

Materials Required for the Unit

Classroom: chart paper, felt pens, pencils, markers, Post-it Notes, metre stick, centimetre rulers, ledger-sized paper, green paper (large, rectangular), pencil crayons, scissors, tape, glue, glue guns, drawing paper, and/or sketch books, green construction paper, dictionaries, writing paper, index cards, coloured pencils, white squares of poster board, glitter pens, paint, paintbrushes, Crayola Model Magic, Plasticine, Styrofoam

Books, Illustrations, and Pictures: fictional storybooks and fairy tales set in medieval times (e.g., *Saint George and the Dragon* as retold by Margaret Hodges, *The Princess and the Pea*, versions of Robin Hood), world map (class size), maps of Europe from the 1200s to modern times (included), feudal system chart (included), pictures of people living in medieval times (included), picture of knight in armour (included), reference material (on knights, armour, heraldry, coats of arms), magazine and calendar pictures of castles, diagram of castle (included), pictures of castles, manor houses, and cottages (included), picture of medieval town (included), picture of medieval church (included), colour prints from illuminated manuscript pages, books about medieval feasts and festivals

Equipment: overhead projector

Other: materials for constructing castle models (cardboard boxes, cylindrical chip cans, milk cartons, string, spools), Lego or building blocks, samples of items that originated in Islamic countries (e.g., black pepper, lemons, rice, sugar, bars of soap, playing cards), wooden dowels, fabric scraps (e.g., satin, brocade, wool, linen, silk), pipe cleaners, food supplies and equipment (will vary depending on menu)

1 | Looking Back in Time

Note: The medieval age may well be a rather abstract idea for young students. Therefore, for students to begin to understand the historical perspective being studied, you may find it best to introduce this unit through literature set in this time period. Although fairy tales and stories such as Robin Hood are not historical fact, they do present an understanding of what life may have been like in medieval society.

Materials

- variety of fictional storybooks set in medieval times (*Saint George and the Dragon*, as retold by Margaret Hodges, is an excellent story to read to students. Others include fairy tales such as *Rapunzel* or *The Princess and the Pea*, and versions of Robin Hood.)
- chart paper
- markers

Activity

Begin by reading aloud one of the selected stories. Throughout the book, discuss characters, settings, and events that take place. List any specific historical terms on chart paper (e.g., *castle, king, knight*). Ask:

- Do you think this story takes place in present time? Why not?
- How was life different then from what it is like now?

Divide the chart paper into two columns. Title one column *Then* and the other column *Now*. Brainstorm ways that life in the story is different from life now, and record students' ideas under each heading. Also discuss ways that life now is the same as it was many years ago (e.g., people still work, they have homes, they have families).

Now discuss the difference between fact and fiction as related to literature. Explain that fiction is a type of story that did not really take place. Ask:

- Do you think that the story we read is fact or fiction? Why?
- What happened in the story that could not happen in real life?
- What happened in the story that could have happened long ago in real life?

Explain that even though the story is fictitious, some parts of the story describe what life was like in medieval times. Record the term *medieval times* on chart paper, and explain to students that they are going to have an opportunity to learn more about real life in medieval times.

Note: To effectively introduce this topic, you may wish to read and discuss several other books set in medieval times.

Activity Sheet A

Directions to students:

On the Venn diagram, use the left circle to record your ideas about what life was like in the story. In the right circle, describe what life is like now. In the intersecting part of the two circles, record ways that life then and life now are the same (1.1.1).

Activity Sheet B

Directions to students:

Record new terms you learn as you study medieval times. Include diagrams, examples, and definitions for each term (1.1.2).

Name: _____

Date: _____

Life Then and Life Now

Story _____

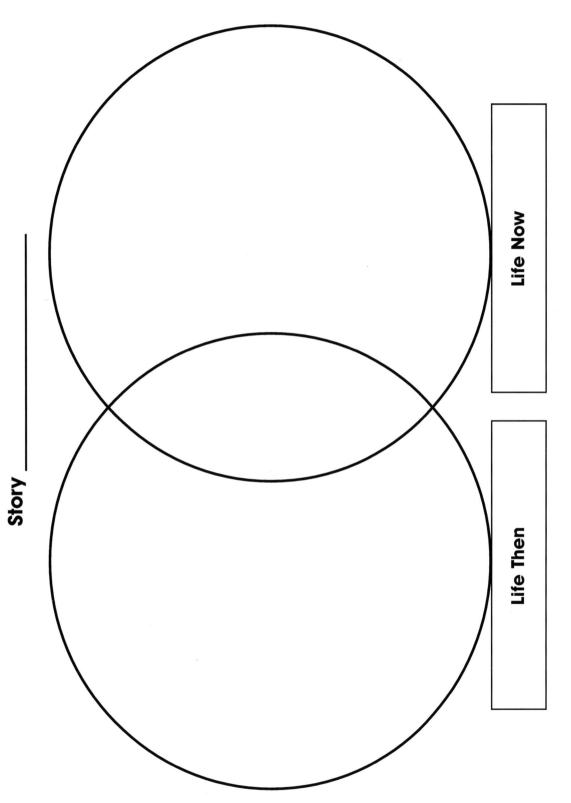

Life Then

Life Now

Glossary

Term	Definitions	Diagrams and Examples

2 | Creating a Time Line

Background Information for Teachers

The Middle Ages, or medieval times, occurred in Europe from 500–1450 C.E. The calendar we use to describe the passage of time is called the Gregorian calendar. It is based on the Julian calendar, created by and named after Julius Caesar.

The Julian year was longer than the solar year by about eleven minutes. As a result, by the late sixteenth century the vernal equinox (first day of spring) was being celebrated several days too early and church holidays were no longer occurring in the appropriate seasons. Pope Gregory instituted changes to the Julian calendar that rectified these problems. He also decided that the starting date of the calendar would be the year that Jesus Christ was believed to have been born.

Note: Because the Gregorian calendar uses the birth of Jesus Christ as its starting date, it has not been adopted world-wide. Many prefer to use C.E. (of common era) and B.C.E. (before common era) when citing years to avoid terminology that reflects one particular religion.

Materials

- chart paper
- markers
- Post-it Notes
- metre stick
- centimetre rulers
- time line made on a long strip of paper (Show centuries marked at every decimetre to 2000 C.E. Each year is equal to one millimetre on this time line.)
- diagram titled, "Time Line Sample" (included) (teacher reference) (1.2.1)

Activity

Note: The purpose of this lesson is to introduce students to the concept of a century, to help them grasp that medieval times occurred long ago, and to place the period in a context of history that they can understand.

Begin by reviewing a story read in the previous lesson. Ask:

- What was life like in the time that this story took place?
- Do you remember what we call this time?

On chart paper, begin a concept web about medieval times. Record the term *medieval times* in the centre of the sheet and circle it. Explain that medieval times is also referred to as the Middle Ages. Record the term *Middle Ages* on the web as well. As a class, brainstorm words and phrases that the students suggest are related to the era (e.g., *king, castle, knight*).

During this activity, discuss the differences between fact and fiction and create the web based on factual aspects of the times.

Note: This differentiating may be challenging for some students; they may not be aware that knights and castles are fact. At the same time, they may not fully understand that medieval characters such as dragons are fictional. These concepts will be clarified as students learn more about life in medieval times. The concept web can be added to throughout the unit, as students expand their knowledge about this historic time.

Following this activity, introduce the medieval times according to its historic era. Display the time line. Ask:

- What year is it now? (mark this on the time line using a Post-it Note)
- How long ago do you think medieval times happened?

2

Explain that medieval times began in or about the year 500. Ask:

- Can you find this year on the time line? (mark this with another Post-it Note)
- Does anyone know how long ago that is? (it is more than 1500 years ago)

Now explain that medieval times ended in about the year 1450. Ask:

- How long ago did it end? (about 550 years ago)

Now have students focus on the term C.E. on the time line. Ask:

- Does anyone know what C.E. refers to?

Explain that over 400 years ago, it was decided that the modern calendar would start with the year Jesus Christ was believed to have been born. Until recently, the Western world referred to all years after the birth of Jesus as A.D. A.D. is the abbreviation for *Anno Domini*, which is Latin for "the year of the Lord." Time before the birth of Jesus was referred to as B.C., which stands for "Before Christ." Today, many people use C.E. (of common era) instead of A.D. and B.C.E. (before common era) instead of B.C.

Note: These may be rather abstract ideas for some young students and, therefore, should be introduced solely for information purposes.

Now introduce the term *century*. Record the term on chart paper and explain that a century is "one hundred years." Relating the term *century* to the term *cents* will help the students understand and remember the concept since there are 100 cents in a dollar. Also use this opportunity to review place value by counting by hundreds to 2000. Ask:

- How many centuries have gone by since the calendar we now use began? (twenty)
- What century are we in now? (twenty-first)

Hand out the activity sheet and explain to the students they will now make their own time line on the paper. Ask:

- Do you have enough room on your paper to make a time line that looks like mine?
- How long do you think my time line is? (measure it using the metre stick)
- How long do you think each century marking is? (10 cm)

Explain to the students that they will need to use a smaller scale to draw their time lines. Provide time for them to discover that on their time line, 1 cm = one century. Have them mark 1 to 20 centimetres on the line, then answer the questions about their time line. (See 1.2.1 for Time Line Sample.)

Activity Sheet

Directions to students:

Complete your time line, then answer the questions (1.2.2).

Extensions

- Use the metre stick to point out that a century is represented on the class time line by ten centimetres. Challenge the students to determine whereabouts on the class time line they were born. Students should identify that they have been alive for approximately one centimetre of the time line. Mark their approximate years of birth on the class time line. This activity will help students to conceptualize long ago ages and the passage of a great deal of time.

- Give students math problems that include dates from medieval times. For example, "If a person was born in 1266 and lived to be 45 years old, in what year did he die?" These kinds of problems will help to reinforce place value and subtraction of numbers up to four places.

2

- Play "What Year Am I?" (e.g., "I am a year during the medieval period. I am greater than 1200 and less than 1450. I am an odd number. I have a zero in the ten's place. What year am I?").

- You might consider marking the nineteenth century as the time of the pioneers in North America, since students are familiar with this time in history from grade three social studies.

Assessment Suggestion

Observe students while they work on their time lines. Focus on their understanding of scale, as well as on their ability to mark centuries at equal distances and label the time line accurately. Use the individual student observations sheet on page 14 to record results.

Time Line Sample

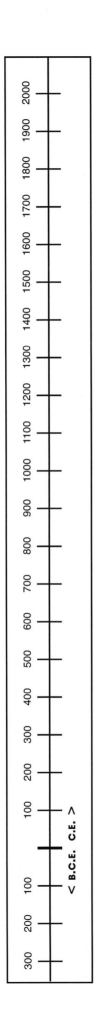

Date: _____

Name: _____

Medieval Time Line

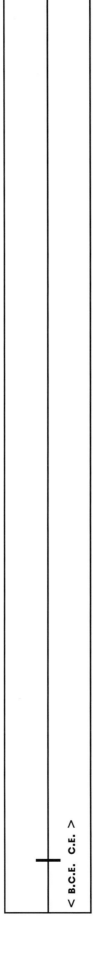

< B.C.E. C.E. >

1. **Mark the centuries on your time line. Use a cm ruler. Start from 100 C.E., and go up to 2000 C.E. How many lines will you need to draw?** _____

2. **Label the centuries on your time line.**

3. **Draw a red vertical line through the date when the medieval period began and the date when it ended.**

4. **How many centuries did the medieval period last?** _____

5. **How many centuries have passed since the medieval period ended?** _____

3 Medieval Europe

Materials

- world map (class size)
- maps of Europe from the 1200s and modern times (included. Make a copy for each student.) (1.3.1, 1.3.2)

Activity

Display the world map. As a class, review the continents of the world. Determine how much background knowledge students have about the continents. Considerable time may have to be spent establishing an understanding of the bodies of land called *continents*. Focus on having the students name the seven continents (North America, South America, Europe, Asia, Africa, Australia, and Antarctica) and identify them on the world map.

Draw attention to Europe, and allow students to observe the large number of countries that make up Europe. Now compare Europe to North America, which has relatively few countries.

Remind students that the time in European history between about 500 and 1450 is referred to as *medieval times*. Ask:

- Do you think that the map of Europe looks the same now as it looked during medieval times?

Hand out the sheets showing a map of Europe from the 1200s (1.3.1) and a modern-day map of Europe (1.3.2). Encourage students to examine the maps carefully and, as a class, discuss things that are different or the same about the two maps.

Now provide students with the activity sheet, and have them compare and contrast the maps, recording their ideas on the sheet.

Activity Sheet

Directions to students:

Carefully examine the maps of Europe – one from the 1200s and the other from modern times. Use the activity sheet to record similarities and differences (1.3.3).

Extensions

- Use Mapmaker Toolkit or other sources to locate a variety of maps of medieval Europe at different dates. Encourage students to identify changes and draw conclusions about the changing boundaries and kingdoms.

- Have students conduct research to find the population of medieval Europe and the population of Europe today, and graph their results.

Europe in 1200 C.E.

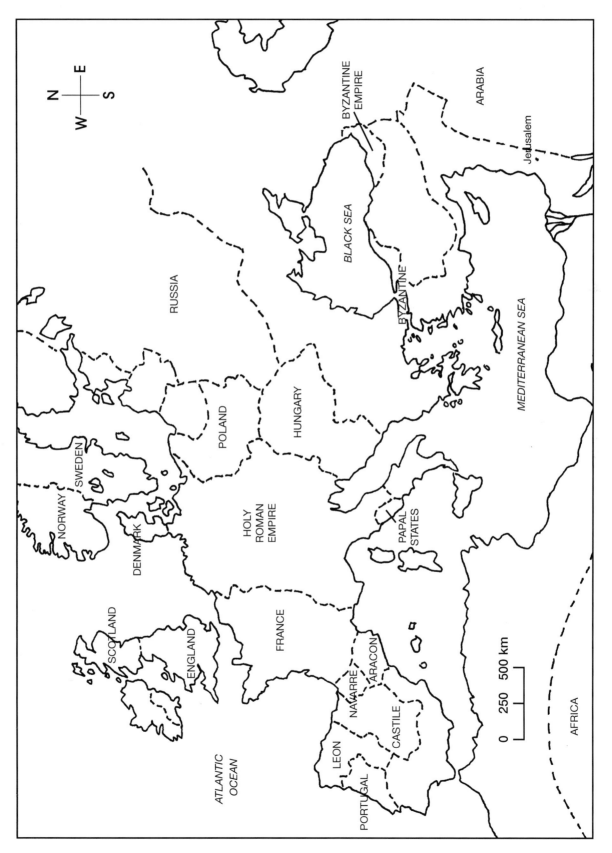

N
E
W ─┼─ S

NORWAY

SWEDEN

DENMARK

RUSSIA

SCOTLAND

ENGLAND

POLAND

HUNGARY

HOLY ROMAN EMPIRE

FRANCE

ATLANTIC OCEAN

PORTUGAL

LEON

NAVARRE

ARACON

CASTILE

PAPAL STATES

BLACK SEA

BYZANTINE EMPIRE

BYZANTINE

MEDITERRANEAN SEA

ARABIA

Jerusalem

AFRICA

0   250   500 km

Present-Day Europe

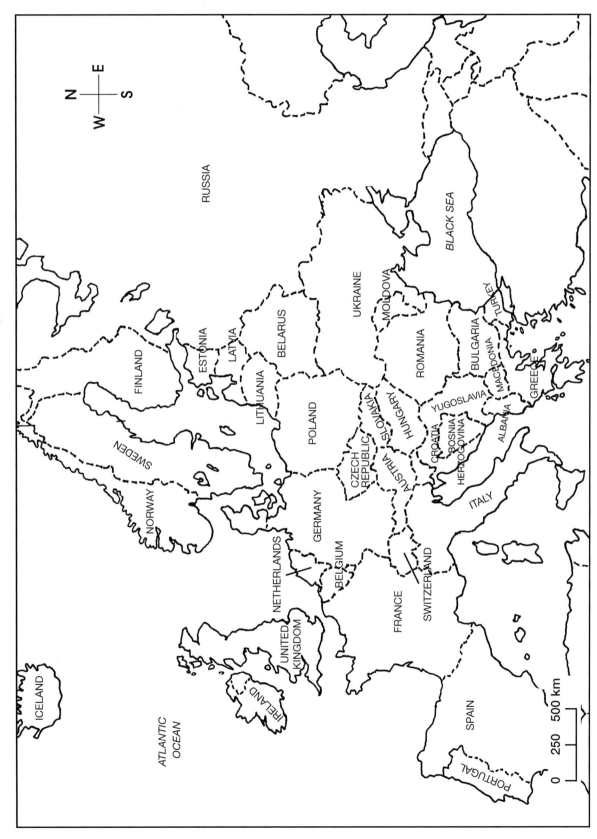

Date:_____   Name: _____

Europe Then and Now

Europe in 1200 C.E.   **Europe in 2000 C.E.**

Differences:

_____   _____

_____   _____

_____   _____

_____   _____

_____   _____

_____   _____

Similarities:

_____   _____

_____   _____

_____   _____

_____   _____

4 The Feudal System

Background Information for Teachers

The Feudal System

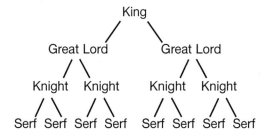

The Middle Ages, or medieval times, began with the fall of the Roman Empire, in about 500. Once the Romans left, there was no strong ruler in charge, so there were no clear laws. From this period onward, there were many invasions and attacks. Land was a means of power during this time, and a king would reward men loyal to him with large parcels of land captured in battles. These parcels of land were called *manors*. Men who swore loyalty to their king and promised to fight for him in return for the land became powerful great lords.

A great lord, in turn, gave smaller manors to knights who were loyal to him and promised to fight for him, if necessary. At the bottom of this hierarchy were the peasants, known as serfs, who were obliged to work for the lord of the manor and fight for him when necessary.

The great lords and the king built large castles to defend their property from invasions. Knights lived in manor houses, and serfs lived in cottages on the manor.

Materials

- chart titled, "Feudal System Hierarchy" (included. Make an overhead transparency of this sheet.) (1.4.1)
- large rectangular sheet of green paper
- Post-it Notes
- scissors
- marker
- tape
- pictures titled, "Medieval Housing" (included. Copy and, prior to the lesson, cut out one king's castle, two sets of great lord's castles, four manor houses, and eight serfs' cottages.) (1.4.2)
- overhead projector

Activity: Part One: The Feudal System

Introduce the feudal system by discussing how rules are followed in the classroom and at school. Ask:

- What are some of the rules we have in the classroom?
- What happens when someone breaks the rules?
- Who is in charge of the classroom?
- Who is in charge of the school?
- What do you think school would be like if there were no rules and no one was in charge?

Following this discussion, focus on rules within the community. Ask:

- What kinds of rules or laws do we follow in our community?
- Who makes sure that the laws are followed?
- What happens to people who break the law?
- What do you think life would be like in our community if there were no police?

Explain to the students that life in medieval Europe was like a community with no law enforcement. There were lots of wars, and many people were killed. Groups of fighting men travelled throughout the countryside raiding farmlands, burning crops, or taking over the land for themselves. Ask:

4

- What do you think people had to do to survive?

Explain that less powerful people (serfs) had no choice but to pay fighting men (knights) to protect them from other fighting men. Payment was in the form of labour – they farmed a knight's land for him. This became known as the *feudal system*. At the top of this system was the king, who owned all the land.

On the overhead, display the chart depicting the feudal system (1.4.1). As a class, read the terms on the chart and discuss what the students know about these terms.

Note: Use the following activity to show how land was divided up in the feudal system. The large sheet of green paper, which represents the land, will be shared among the different levels of landowners (as described in the activity below).

Note: In Activity: Part Two, homes will be added to this land display to show how dwellings differed at each level of the feudal system.

Display the large rectangle of green paper, and explain that it represents land. Tape it to the classroom wall. Explain that the king owned all the land. On a Post-it Note, write the word *king* and place it below the sheet of green paper.

Now explain that after a successful battle, the king rewarded loyal noblemen who fought for him with large estates, or parcels of land, called *manors*. In exchange for control over their land, the noblemen promised to fight for the king in battles. They also paid taxes to the king for the use of his land.

Cut off two rectangular pieces from each end of the large green sheet (each about 1/4 of the full sheet). Tape these two pieces below the original piece. The noblemen were now very rich and powerful because they had control of lots of land. They were great lords. Record the

term *great lord* on Post-it Notes, and place the notes underneath these two pieces of land.

Each great lord, in turn, gave a section of his manor to men who fought for him. These men were called *knights*. In return for control over their land, the knights promised to fight for their lord when called upon. They also paid taxes to their lord.

Cut off two rectangular pieces from each end of each great lord's land (each about 1/4 of the great lord's land), and tape two pieces below each great lord's land. Write *knight* on Post-it Notes and place beneath these four pieces of land.

Explain that the poorest people were called *serfs*. Serfs did not have their own land. Instead, they worked for the knights. They farmed his land and did other jobs for him in exchange for a place to live and protection from invaders. Sometimes, however, serfs would have to fight for the knights in war. Because serfs had little or no money, they paid taxes usually in the form of loaves of bread or other things they could supply for the knights. Write the term *serf* on several Post-it Notes and place these below the knights' land.

Review the chart of the feudal system, along with the display made of the land. Encourage the students to describe the feudal system in their own words.

Now have the students complete the activity sheet and describe their understanding of the feudal system.

Activity Sheet

Directions to students:

Fill in the chart of the feudal system. Write a sentence to describe each level of the system (1.4.2).

4

Activity: Part Two: Homes in the Feudal System

Review the chart of the feudal system, along with the display made of the land. Using the information sheet titled, "Medieval Housing," cut out one king's castle, two great lord's castles, four manor houses, and eight serf's cottages (1.4.3). Ask:

- Who is at the top of the feudal system?
- Who is at the bottom?
- Do you think life was the same for the king as it was for the serfs?
- What do you think the king's home was like?
- What was the king's home called?

Tape the picture of the king's castle onto the green paper (land) belonging to the king. Explain that the king lived in a large castle made of stone. Ask:

- Where do you think the great lords lived?

Explain that, like the king, the great lords were rich and powerful. They also lived in castles. They could have as many castles as they had parcels of land. They often had to move from castle to castle to guard their land. Place pictures of the great lords' castles on the green paper (land) belonging to the great lords.

Now focus on the knights. Ask:

- What do you notice about the size of property that each knight controlled? (It is much smaller than the property of his great lord.)
- What type of home do you think a knight lived in?

If students suggest a castle, acknowledge that some knights were wealthy enough to build a castle, but it was much smaller than his great lord's castle. Most knights lived in houses called *manor houses*. A manor house was made of stone and had two floors. Tape a picture of a manor house on each piece of green paper (land) owned by a knight. Ask:

- Do you think serfs lived in manor houses?

Allow students the opportunity to discuss their opinions and to explain their reasoning.

Tape pictures of the serfs' cottages along the bottom of the display beneath the Post-it Notes labelled *serf*. Explain that a serf's cottage had only one or two rooms and was made of thatch, twigs, and mud. Ask:

- Which home would you prefer to live in? Why?
- Which home is most like the homes we live in today?

Extensions

- Have students use notebooks or bound sheets of paper to develop a glossary of medieval terms. Encourage them to list all of the words that were introduced in this lesson and to describe each term in their own words. Have them add to this glossary throughout the unit.

- Have students reflect on and discuss how medieval society is different from present-day society (e.g., no kings and knights, no feudal system). Also, discuss societal similarities (e.g., people with more/less power, poor and wealthy people, and so on).

Assessment Suggestion

Have students use their activity sheet to give an explanation of the feudal system in their own words. Use the individual student observations sheet on page 14 to record results.

Feudal System Hierarchy

```
                        ┌──────────────────┐
                        │                  │
                        │       King       │
                        │                  │
                        └──────────────────┘

      ┌────────────┐                          ┌────────────┐
      │   Great    │                          │   Great    │
      │    Lord    │                          │    Lord    │
      └────────────┘                          └────────────┘

  ┌────────┐   ┌────────┐              ┌────────┐   ┌────────┐
  │ Knight │   │ Knight │              │ Knight │   │ Knight │
  └────────┘   └────────┘              └────────┘   └────────┘

┌──────┐┌──────┐┌──────┐┌──────┐  ┌──────┐┌──────┐┌──────┐┌──────┐
│ Serf ││ Serf ││ Serf ││ Serf │  │ Serf ││ Serf ││ Serf ││ Serf │
└──────┘└──────┘└──────┘└──────┘  └──────┘└──────┘└──────┘└──────┘
```

The Feudal System

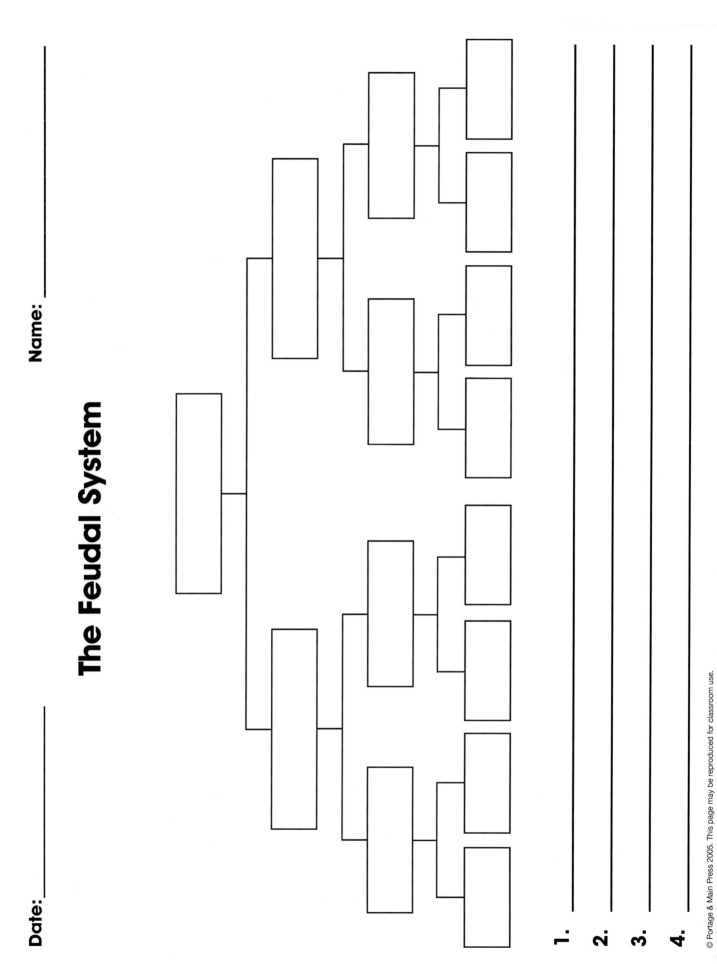

1. _____

2. _____

3. _____

4. _____

Medieval Housing

King's castle

Great Lord's castle

Knight's manor house

Serf's cottage

5 The Nobility – Kings, Great Lords, and Ladies

Background Information for Teachers

In medieval society, members of the nobility were those who had been given titles by the king, controlled land, or were born into a family with titles and land.

Nobility included kings, great lords, ladies, and knights.

Materials

- chart paper
- marker
- chart of the feudal system and the land display (from lesson 4)
- illustration titled "Nobles, Knights, and Serfs" (included. Make a copy for each student.) (1.5.1)
- information sheet titled, "A Great Lord" (included. Make a copy for each student.) (1.5.2)
- information sheet titled, "The Lady of the Manor" (included. Make a copy for each student.) (1.5.3)
- overhead projector

Activity: Part One: Identifying the Nobility

Begin by reviewing the feudal system, as presented in the previous lesson. Ask:

- Who was at the top of the feudal system?

On chart paper, record the term *king*. Ask:

- What do you know about kings of medieval times?
- Where did they live?
- How did they dress?
- How did they live?
- What kinds of activities were they involved in?

On the chart paper, record all of the students' ideas about kings.

Note: This chart may be added to in future lessons as students learn more about medieval times.

Display the chart of the feudal system from the previous lesson. Ask:

- Who was next in order in the feudal system?
- Which groups owned most of the land?
- Which groups were wealthy?
- Which groups were poor?

Explain that people with wealth and power were called *nobility*. They included kings, great lords, knights, and their families. Record the term *nobility* on chart paper.

Distribute the picture of people (1.5.1) from medieval times. Ask:

- What do you notice about the people in these pictures?
- Who do you think they are?
- Are there any nobility in these pictures?
- Which people do you think are nobility? Why?
- Are there any serfs in the pictures?
- How do you know they are serfs?

Focus on the people that the students have identified as nobility. Ask:

- So far, what do you know about the people who belonged to the nobility?
- What types of activities do they seem to be engaged in?

Record valid points on the chart, and explain to students that they will learn more about the nobility by reading a story about a great lord and a story about his lady.

Hand out the information sheets (1.5.2, 1.5.3), and read each aloud while students follow along on their own copies. Ask:

- What have you learned about nobility?
- What would life be like as a great lord?
- What would life be like as a lady?

5

- Would you like to have been a great lord or lady in medieval Europe?

Following this discussion, distribute the activity sheet, and have students describe what they think would be advantages and disadvantages to being a great lord or lady in medieval times.

Activity Sheet

Directions to students:

List, in point form, all the advantages you can think of about being a lord and lady in medieval times. List any disadvantages you can think of for each (1.5.4).

Extensions

- Have students examine art from medieval times. (Some can be found on the Internet, in calendars, or in school art kits. The New York Metropolitan Museum of Art sells cards, calendars, and address books illustrated with medieval prints.) Challenge

the students to identify nobility and other people in various levels of the feudal system. They can use clues based on the peoples' dress and activities to identify who they might be.

- Have students research Eleanor of Aquitaine. She was a very interesting noblewoman and the queen of France and England at different times in her life. Students can present their research to the class.

Activity Centre

Display pictures of kings, lords, ladies, and their children. Have students use reference books and web sites to find examples of the clothing worn by these people in medieval times. They can then use the paper doll outlines on the activity centre sheets (1.5.5) to create figures of lords and ladies and their children. The paper dolls can then be used as characters in plays about medieval nobility.

Nobles, Knights, and Serfs

A Great Lord

Meet the great lord, Sir Hugh, baron of many manors. Hugh was born into a noble family. His father was a baron who helped the king win a great battle and take over many lands. The king rewarded Hugh's father by giving him the title of baron and control over many manors. When Hugh's father died, Hugh inherited his father's estates and his title.

Life has not always been easy for Hugh. He has fought for the king many times in his thirty-three years. Many of his fellow knights have died in battle. Hugh first learned about battle when he was only a young boy. He left his family at the age of seven to begin the long training to become a knight.

Sir Hugh has many other responsibilities besides going to war for his king. He must oversee the operation of all his castles and manors. To help him, he has a steward who takes care of the finances of his castles.

Sir Hugh begins each day with prayers in the castle chapel, then he eats breakfast. He then meets with his steward to hear about the business of the manor. He knows very little about how to run a farm, so he relies on his steward and his wife, Lady Jane, to manage these affairs. Lady Jane is Sir Hugh's second wife. His first wife died in childbirth; the baby died as well.

Later, Sir Hugh listens to his bailiff tell him the crimes committed by some of the serfs. Hugh is the voice of the king on the manor – he decides guilt or innocence and what punishment should be given for each crime.

For entertainment, Sir Hugh enjoys hunting with his dogs in his forests and hunting with trained hawks and falcons. He also enjoys feasting with his friends and attending the court of the king in his castle.

The Lady of the Manor

Meet Lady Jane, baroness of many manors. Like her husband, Lady Jane was born into a noble family. If she had not been, Hugh would never have arranged with her family for the marriage. Their parents wanted a marriage that would join their families in land and wealth. Most important, Hugh wished for a male heir to inherit his land and title. Jane had not really met Hugh until it was almost time to be married. She was only fourteen—eleven years younger than her husband. Nobles did not marry for love.

Lady Jane has a busy day in the castle. She must organize the servants and be sure everything is prepared for the arrival of some noble guests. For fun, Jane rides her horse and takes part in a sport called falconry with her husband and their friends.

Jane will soon say goodbye to her husband. Sir Hugh will be leaving with their guests in a day or two to join the king in battle. With his skills on the battlefield, Jane hopes he survives and brings honour to his family. While he is away Jane will inspect the local farms, make sure the servants of the castle see to needed repairs, and oversee the clothes making by inspecting the weaving and meeting with the tailors. She teaches her daughter embroidery and how to run a household. Her son is eight years old and has gone to serve as page to his aunt and uncle who live on a manor far away. He is learning to become a knight like his father. (Jane lost her third child before he was two years old, due to illness.)

Would You Like to Be a Great Lord or Lady?

List the advantages and disadvantages of being a great lord in medieval times.

Advantages	Disadvantages

List the advantages and disadvantages of being a great lady in medieval times.

Advantages	Disadvantages

Paper Doll Cutouts

Date: _____

Adult Female

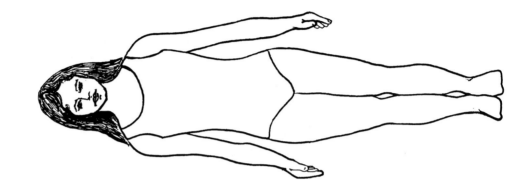

Adult Male

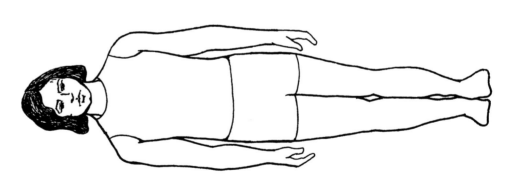

Paper Doll Cutouts

Female Child

Male Child

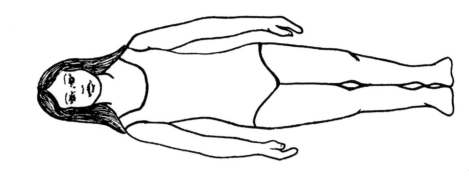

6 The Nobility – Knights

Note: The student information sheets and activity sheets included with this lesson provide details on the process of becoming a knight, as well as the design of a knight's coat of arms.

Materials

- information sheet titled, "The Long Journey to Becoming a Knight" (included. Make a copy for each student.) (1.6.1)
- diagram titled, "Knight in Armour" (included. Make an overhead transparency of this sheet.) (1.6.3)
- diagram titled, "Coats of Arms" (included. Make an overhead transparency of this sheet. You may choose to colour in the coat of arms using reference material as a guide.) (1.6.4)
- overhead projector
- reference material on knights, armour, heraldry, and coats of arms
- pencil crayons (various colours)

Activity: Part One: Becoming a Knight

Begin by reviewing the roles of nobility, specifically the role of the great lords. Explain, for example, that Sir Hugh (see lesson 5) did not become a knight simply because his father had been one. Ask:

- What did he have to do to become a knight?

Discuss students' ideas. Divide the class into groups of four students. Hand out the information sheet "The Long Journey to Becoming a Knight" (1.6.1). Have the students in each group select a page to read (Readers A, B, C, D), while the others follow along.

Once the groups have finished reading, discuss being a page, a squire, and a knight. Use this information to identify the roles of the people in the illustrations on the information sheet.

Following this discussion, distribute Activity Sheet A (1.6.2). Have the students complete the sheet based on what they have learned about knights.

Activity Sheet A

Directions to students:

Read the statements and write *page, squire,* or *knight* beside each one (1.6.2).

Activity: Part Two: Heraldry and the Coat of Arms

On the overhead, display the diagram of the knight in armour (1.6.3). Ask:

- Who is this?
- Why would a knight be dressed like this?
- What is the outfit called?
- What is the purpose of the armour?

Review the armour parts and discuss how these protect a knight during battle. Ask:

- Can you see the knight's face?
- How do you think the knights could tell who were their friends and who were their enemies?

Explain that knights used a special design called a *coat of arms* on their tunic and shield so they could identify and be identified by others. Each knight designed his own coat of arms. Display the overhead of the coats of arms and discuss the designs and symbols used (1.6.4). Ask:

- What shape is a coat of arms?
- How are the coats of arms different?
- What symbols and designs are used?
- What would your coat of arms look like if you had one?

6

Provide reference material on heraldry and coats of arms, along with Activity Sheet B (1.6.5). Have students examine the various designs, symbols, and colours used. Provide students with plenty of time to design their coats of arms.

Activity Sheet B

Note: This is a two-page activity sheet.

Directions to students:

Choose symbols for your coat of arms. Families were very important to knights. Think about your family. Is there a symbol that comes to mind that describes it – perhaps a symbol to show your mother's or father's occupation? You might decide to include a symbol that stands for a special talent or interest you have. Record your symbols and what they mean on the first page, then use the coat of arms outline to design your own family coat of arms (1.6.5).

Extensions

■ Read tales of King Arthur to the class and discuss the qualities of knighthood that are described in these stories. There are many easy-to-read versions of King Arthur. Students could read the tales in literature circles and discuss evidence of chivalry they find in the story. Explain to students that although the stories of King Arthur were set in an earlier time, they were made up and retold by the people of medieval times. Therefore, they describe a lot of the elements of medieval times.

■ Find illustrations of armour from different centuries and regions of medieval Europe. Have students compare them and determine which would be more effective during battle.

■ Draw examples of armour. Visit museums in your area that have displays of armour. Bring sketchbooks, draw samples, and take notes on observations.

■ Research types of weapons used by knights. Illustrate the weapons, and present to the class.

The Long Journey to Becoming a Knight

Reader A:

In families of nobility, wealth and titles were passed down from fathers to sons. A boy did not inherit the title of knight, however; he had to earn it.

The Page

The path to knighthood started at a very early age. When a boy born into a noble family turned seven he said goodbye to his family and went to live in a different castle with strangers. First, he had to be trained as a page. As page, he served the lord and lady their meals, ran errands, and studied reading, writing, and mathematics. He was taught manners, and practiced the art of hunting and fighting. The page learned archery, sword-play using wooden swords, and how to use other weapons. He spent most of his time learning fighting skills; very little of his time was spent learning to read and write. Most knights could do little more than read and write their own name.

Reader B:

The Squire

When a page turned fourteen, he embarked on the hardest part of his training. He became a squire and was assigned to a knight. The squire served his knight by looking after his knight's armour, polishing it, and helping his knight put his heavy armour on. A squire also looked after weapons, fed the war horse, and made sure the horse was kept in the best condition. Squires had to complete tests of endurance. One test was to go twenty-four hours without food or water. Another, more difficult, test was to go three or four days without food. The squire went with his knight to tournaments. There, knights competed with other knights for money or armour. Tournaments were an important way for knights to practice battle skills in times of peace. A squire spent most of his time in or around the castle practicing with weapons and learning how to fight. The squire, then, was prepared to go to war with his knight. Sadly, many squires died in battle while they were still teenagers.

Reader C:

The Dubbing Ceremony

Worthy squires were usually knighted by the time they were twenty-one. The evening before he was to become a knight, the squire was washed and shaved and taken to the chapel. He stayed in the chapel all night, praying for guidance to be a good knight. The next day, after breakfast with his family and friends, the dubbing ceremony took place in the great hall of the castle. The lord or king picked up the young man's sword, tapped his right shoulder three times with the blade of the sword, and said, "In the name of God, I dub thee knight." From then on, he had the title "Sir" before his name.

After the ceremony, the newly anointed knight returned to the chapel where he was blessed by the priest. At the celebration that followed, the new knight presented gifts to the church and to the peasants who had come to watch the ceremony.

Reader D:

Chivalry

This word originally meant "horsemanship," but soon came to mean much more. It became a code of behaviour for knights to follow. Knights were expected to display certain qualities in the code of chivalry:

- A knight must be honourable and brave.
- A knight must protect the weak, and respect women.
- A knight must be loyal to the king.

Page, Squire, or Knight?

1. People call me "Sir" wherever I go.   _____

2. I look after my knight's horse.   _____

3. I have to go 24 hours with no food or water.   _____

4. I had to leave my family when I was only
   seven years old.   _____

5. I promised to be honourable and brave.   _____

6. I serve the lord and lady their meals.   _____

7. I study reading and writing, but mostly
   I learn how to hunt and fight.   _____

8. I look after the knight's armour and
   weapons.   _____

9. I compete in tournaments for practice
   when there are no wars to fight.   _____

10. I may have to go to war with my knight.   _____

11. I was dubbed by the king. It was a special
    moment in my life.   _____

Knight in Armour

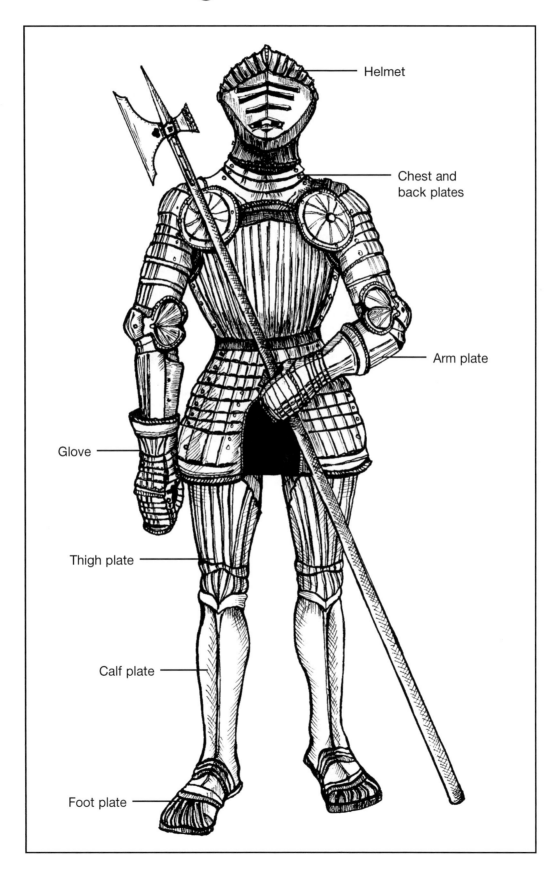

Helmet

Chest and
back plates

Arm plate

Glove

Thigh plate

Calf plate

Foot plate

Coats of Arms

Coat of Arms

Knights decorated their shields and tunics with a special badge so that fellow knights and squires would recognize them in battle. The designing of this personal badge is called *heraldry*. The badge is called a *coat of arms*.

Every part of the coat of arms was a symbol of something in the knight's life. For example, a knight who was the third son born in his family would use a star, and the fourth son would use a bird as one of the symbols on his coat of arms. Symbols from the father's and mother's coats of arms were also used in the knight's design. The colours used were gold, silver, blue, red, black, green, and purple.

Design your own coat of arms. Think about yourself and your family. Choose symbols for your coat of arms, and describe what each symbol means:

Symbol	What It Means

Date:_____   Name: _____

My Coat of Arms

7 | The Castle

Materials

- KWL chart (Divide chart paper into three columns: *What We Know About Castles, What We Want to Know About Castles, What We Learned About Castles.*)
- markers
- chart paper
- pictures of castles (Calendars of castles are inexpensive if purchased in the New Year. Pictures can also be downloaded off many web sites.)

Note: The more pictures of castles you collect, the better. Students will use them in a variety of ways.

- illustration titled, "A Stone Castle" (included. Make an overhead transparency of this sheet.) (1.7.1)
- overhead projector
- books about castles and medieval life
- information sheet titled, "Important Features of a Medieval Castle" (included. Make a copy for each student.) (1.7.2)
- materials for constructing models of castles (e.g., cardboard boxes, cylindrical chip cans, milk cartons, masking tape, strings and spools for pulleys on drawbridge)
- Post-it Notes

Activity: Part One: Determining Prior Knowledge

Begin the lesson by discussing and recording what students already know about castles. Ask:

- What do you know about castles?

Record all responses in the first column of the KWL chart. Accept all responses; however, if some students object to another's fact, put a question mark beside the fact. These statements can be checked throughout the lesson as students learn more about castles. Ask:

- Can you think of anything you would like to know about castles?

Write down students' questions in the second column of the chart. You may need to prompt the students to consider why castles were built, who actually built them, what they were like inside, how comfortable they were, and so on.

Note: The KWL chart can be completed throughout the unit as students learn more about castles.

Activity: Part Two: Observing the Structure of Castles

Arrange the class into groups of four or five students. Provide each group with several castle pictures, along with chart paper and markers. Have the groups examine each picture, and record their observations on the chart paper. Have the groups share their observations. Now challenge each group to sort the pictures, and have other groups guess the sorting rules used by each.

Following the sorting activity, ask:

- Why do you think people of medieval times started building castles?

Remind the students that there were many kingdoms in medieval times, and invaders were constantly attacking, raiding and burning farmlands, and taking over the land. Ask:

- Why do you think the king and his lords started building castles? (easy to defend)
- What do you notice about the castles? (large wall around edge, moat, gate/drawbridge, towers, and so on)
- How would these features help to protect the castle and its inhabitants from invaders?

Display the overhead of the castle (1.7.1) on the overhead projector. Discuss the design of the castle, features observed, and challenge students to determine why the features are important.

Explain that although all castles were different, some features common to most meant the castle was a safe place to be during attacks.

Note: Location was very important when deciding where to build a castle. Many are located at the top of hills so potential attackers could be easily seen and the castle defended.

Distribute activity sheet A (1.7.3), along with the information sheet on castles (1.7.2). Have the students use the information to identify and label the features of a castle.

Activity Sheet A

Directions to students:

Read the description of castle features again. Label the features on your diagram (1.7.3).

Activity: Part Three: Identifying Parts of Castles

Divide the class into working groups, and have the groups examine the pictures of castles again (1.7.1). Provide them with Post-it Notes, and have them use the castle information sheet along with activity sheet A to identify the castles' features. They can record the name of each feature on a Post-it Note and stick it directly on the picture.

Note: Remind students that the pictures are of actual castles. Some may be of castle ruins, in which case all features may not be identifiable. Also, no two castles were alike. There were many different styles of castles, depending on the time period and area. Students may not recognize every feature in every picture.

Activity: Part Four: Constructing a Castle Model

Note: This activity could be integrated with the *Hands-On Science* module *Pulleys and Gears*.

Divide the class into working groups. Explain that they will design and construct their own

model of a castle with a drawbridge. Give students time to plan and design their castle, using activity sheet B. They may also require additional time to gather the necessary materials. Once the groups have made their plans, have them construct their castles and test their drawbridge designs. Modifications may be required throughout the process.

Provide an opportunity for students to share their castle projects with their peers, other classes, and families.

Activity Sheet B

Note: This is a two-page activity sheet.

Directions to students:

Plan and design your castle (1.7.4).

Extensions

■ Research methods that were used to defend castles.

■ Research famous castles of the world, and find out where they are located.

■ Divide the class into groups to research different features of castles; for example, furniture in the castle, the lord and lady's quarters, the dungeons, the kitchen, the great hall. Groups can share their information with the class, or prepare a poster display of their research to be displayed in the classroom.

■ Brainstorm words to describe castles. Encourage interesting adjectives. Students can use these words to write haiku or other forms of poetry about castles.

■ Have students staple together several sheets of drawing paper and title the booklet *Medieval Sketchbook*. Give the students many opportunities to sketch castles from the photographs. After many drawings, have students choose their best drawing to develop into a project to display. Here are several to choose from:

- Go over the castle lines with permanent felt marker, then use watercolours to complete the picture.
- Go over the castle lines with water-soluble marker. Take a clean, wet brush and pull it along the lines of the castle to accent the drawing. The ink from the marker will bleed into the water, creating a painting of the work.
- With pencil, draw a castle on black construction paper. Drizzle white glue over each line and leave it to dry. The drawing now has clear, shiny lines where the pencil marks were. Have the students use chalk pastels to colour their castle. The glue lines will not hold chalk, but will define the shape of the castle. Encourage students to blend colours for a more interesting effect.

Assessment Suggestions

- As students work in their groups to sort and label the castle pictures, observe their ability to work together. Use the cooperative skills teacher assessment sheet on page 18 to record results.

- Have students complete the cooperative skills self-assessment sheet on page 20 to reflect on their ability to work in a group setting.

- As a class, identify criteria for the castle models. These may include:
  - clear, labelled plan
  - sturdy construction
  - working drawbridge
  - ability to identify key parts and explain use

  List these criteria on the rubric on page 16 and record results.

A Stone Castle

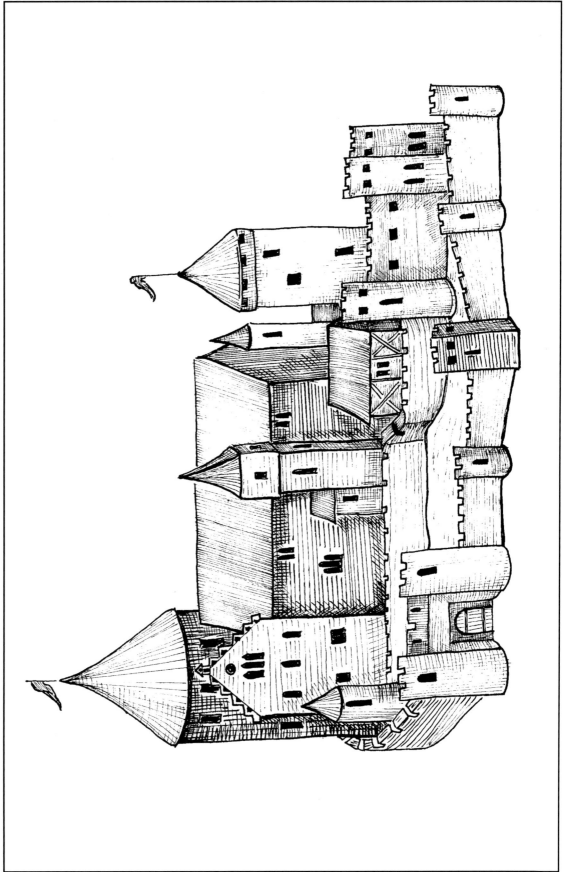

Important Features of a Medieval Castle

The Keep: The highest point in the castle. It was the strongest part of the castle, with walls up to 7 metres thick. The king's quarters, the guest rooms, and the great hall were all within the keep. In the basement of the keep were the dungeons, where prisoners were kept.

Gatehouse: A building that protected the entrance to the castle, usually with a tower at either side. The gate, drawbridge, and portcullis were found here.

Outer Walls: The walls that surrounded the castle grounds.

Wall Walk: The area at the top of the outer wall where soldiers defending the castle could walk along and look out on all sides of the castle.

Bailey: The large open area inside the castle walls. The kitchen, stables, work areas, and storage sheds were found here.

Portcullis: A heavy gate made of iron. The portcullis was raised and lowered by pulleys.

Moat and Drawbridge: The moat, a large ditch or trench usually filled with water, surrounded the castle's outer walls. The drawbridge, used to cross the moat, was made of heavy wood. It was raised and lowered by pulleys.

Date: _____

Name: _____

Important Features
of a Medieval Castle

Label parts of the castle using these terms:
keep, gatehouse, outer walls, wall walk, bailey, portcullis, moat, drawbridge

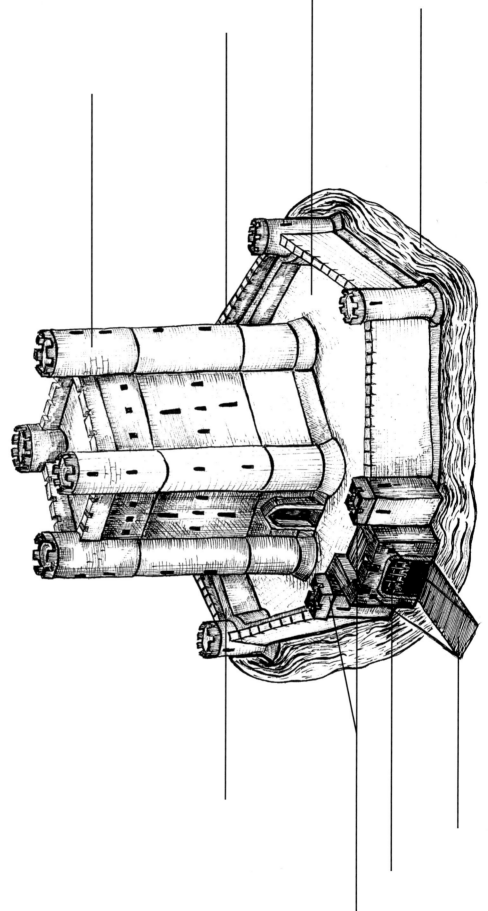

Date:_____   Name: _____

_____

_____

_____

Castle Plan

1. Draw a labelled diagram of your castle design. Be sure you have included these parts on your castle:

Gatehouse   **Outer walls**   **Bailey**
Keep   **Drawbridge**

2. Materials Required

_____   _____   _____

_____   _____   _____

_____   _____   _____

_____   _____   _____

_____   _____   _____

3. Now build your castle model. Test the drawbridge.

4. List any modifications to your design.

_____

_____

_____

5. Draw the final product.

8 | Who Else Worked in a Castle?

Background Information for Teachers

A great variety of people worked in a medieval castle. They included:

Atilliator: made crossbows

Butlet: worked in the cellar; in charge of the butts (bottles) of wine and beer

Cottar: the lowest of the peasantry who worked as swineherdsmen, prison guards, and at odd jobs

Falconer: cared for and trained the hawks for the sport of falconry

Porter: took care of the doors, especially the main entrance

Steward: supervised the household and castle events

Note: Many common surnames of British heritage derived from actual jobs done in or around castles and manors in medieval times. For example, Hayward was someone who tended the hedges. Carter was a workman who brought wood and stone to the castle building site. A man named Robert, who had the job of Carter, was referred to as Robert, the Carter, and eventually just as Robert Carter.

Materials

- chart paper
- markers
- reference books and bookmarked web sites about castles

Activity

Begin by discussing castle ownership. Ask:

- Did everyone own a castle in medieval times?
- Who owned castles?
- Where did other people live?

Review that the king and the great lords owned and lived in the castles. Ask:

- Do you think that the king or nobleman took care of the castle himself?
- Who else might have worked in a castle?

List students' suggestions on chart paper.

Have pairs of students read books together about people who lived and worked in castles, and to find out the names of their occupations. Add these names to the list on chart paper. Be sure to include workers such as stewards, bailiffs, servants, cooks, stable keepers, dungeon guards; as well as entertainers such as jesters, jugglers, and minstrels.

Provide students with the activity sheet. Have them choose interesting jobs from the list and write a description of it on the activity sheet.

Activity Sheet

Directions to students:

Choose two castle jobs from the class list. Find out what these jobs involved, and fill out the description sheet. You may illustrate your job descriptions as well (1.8.1).

Extension

Use the extension activity sheet to create a message describing the jobs available in the castle, and choose a town crier in the class to announce them (1.8.2).

Castle Jobs

Name: _____

Date: _____

Castle Job: _____

Description: _____

_____
_____
_____

Would you want this job?

Yes   No

Why? _____

_____
_____
_____
_____

Name: _____

Castle Job: _____

Description: _____

_____
_____
_____

Would you want this job?

Yes   No

Why? _____

_____
_____
_____
_____

Name: _____

Available Jobs

Hear ye, hear ye!

**The following jobs need-st be filled
at the great castle...**

9 The Manor System

Background Information for Teachers

In the manor system, a knight was lord of the manor. The manor itself generally consisted of farmland organized in strips, a river or stream, a mill where grain was ground into flour, a well, the manor house, serf cottages, and forest land.

Knights were not all equally wealthy. Only first-born sons inherited their father's lands and titles. Other sons inherited nothing, and so hired themselves out as knights to great lords. These knights lived in the great lord's castle, or travelled from place to place fighting for lords who would pay them.

Serfs were, essentially, slaves. The word *serf* comes from the Latin word for "slave." Serfs could leave the manor only if they bought their freedom or escaped and were not caught for two years. Freed serfs were called *villeins* or *peasants*. It is debatable whether or not they were better off than the serfs. Many had no land to farm and ended up as beggars in the villages; some became serfs again.

Materials

- chart of the feudal system (from lesson 4)
- land display of the feudal system (from lesson 4)
- picture titled, "Manor House" (included. Make an overhead transparency of this sheet.) (1.9.1)
- overhead projector
- information sheet titled, "The Manor System" (included. Make a copy for each student.) (1.9.2)
- picture titled, "Serf's Cottage" (included. Make an overhead transparency of this sheet.) (1.9.5)
- story titled, *Life as a Serf* (included) (for teacher use only) (1.9.4)

Activity: Part One: The Manor System

Review the feudal system. Ask:

- Who is at the top of the feudal system? (king)
- Who else owns castles? (great lords)
- Where do knights live? (manor houses)
- Who is at the bottom of the feudal system? (serfs)

Remind the students that although knights are considered nobility, not every nobleman lived in a castle. Many knights owned a piece of land called a *manor* and lived in a manor house. Ask:

- Who did the work on the manor?
- What did the lord of the manor do?

Explain that the way people lived and worked on the manor was called *the manor system.* Display the overhead of the manor house (1.9.1). Ask:

- What do you notice about the manor house?
- How is it different from a castle?

Distribute the information sheet (1.9.2) about the manor system and, as a class, read it. Now distribute activity sheet A (1.9.3), which describes the manor house. Have the students use this information, along with the overhead, to draw a diagram of the manor house.

Activity Sheet A

Directions to students:

Use the information on the sheet to help you as you draw a diagram of a manor house (1.9.3).

▶

9

Activity: Part Two: Life as a Serf

Ask students to describe what life might have been like for the serfs who lived and worked on the manor. As a class, discuss their ideas.

Read the information sheet "Life as a Serf" (1.9.4) to the students. As you read, have students sit comfortably, close their eyes, and imagine what life was like.

Following this reading, invite students to discuss details they recall from the story. Ask:

- How is life for serfs different from life for noble families?

Emphasize that serfs, while poor, had an important benefit. The land they lived on belonged to the lord of the manor, and they were promised protection from raiders and plunderers – enemies were more hesitant to attack estates than they were to attack open strips of land.

Display the overhead of the serf's cottage (1.9.5). Have students describe what they notice about the cottage. For example:

- no proper fireplace, just a pit with smoke going toward a hole in the roof
- only one or two rooms
- stable is inside the cottage
- not much furniture

Discuss what materials we used to construct a serf's cottage (e.g., reeds, mud, twigs, timber), and compare to the materials used to build a manor house (e.g., stone, wood). These materials were all from the natural environment and were easily accessible. People used only materials that were accessible in their geographical area.

Provide each student with activity sheet B (1.9.6). As a class, read the description of the serf's cottage, then have students complete the sheet. Discuss their ideas and responses.

Activity Sheet B

Note: This is a two-page activity sheet.

Directions to students:

Read about the serf's cottage, then answer the questions (1.9.6).

Activity: Part Three: Past and Present Compared

Discuss how manor life is different from life in your community. Allow students the opportunity to discuss this over time. Bring the question up after each new element of medieval society is explored so that students will have a fuller understanding of the ways the two societies are different and the ways they are the same.

Following each discussion, have students reflect on their learning by recording ideas on the Venn diagram on activity sheet C (1.9.7). Discuss students' ideas to identify similarities and differences between medieval society and present-day life in your community.

Activity Sheet C

Directions to students:

On the outside circles, record the differences between medieval society and your society. On the intersection, record similarities between the two societies. Write three statements about the ideas on your Venn diagram (1.9.7).

Manor House

The Manor System

In medieval times, most people in Europe were serfs who lived on the estates of nobles. The serfs worked the land and gave the lords part of their crops. In return, the serfs were under the protection of the lord.

The manor house and the village church were the largest buildings on the manor. There were about twenty or thirty cottages for the serfs. Nearby, there were usually a stream or river, crop fields, and forest land that had not been cleared.

Crop fields were planted with different grains or vegetables. The fields were divided into thin, long strips of farmland. Each strip was farmed by a serf and his family. Many of these strips were for the lord, and each serf would help to work his lord's land. A smaller amount of land was left for each serf to farm for himself.

All the food had to be grown on the manor. Beans and peas were grown and dried to store for wintertime. Hay was grown to feed animals over winter. Most animals were butchered in the fall because there was not enough food to feed them over the winter. The meat was salted to prevent it from spoiling quickly. It would be eaten throughout the winter.

The Manor House

A manor house was surrounded by a stone wall to protect the family inside from enemies. The manor house was made of stone as well, and usually had two floors. The family lived on the top floor. There were usually three rooms and a chapel on this floor. The family used the chapel for prayers and was often visited by the manor priest. A fireplace heated the house, and there could be more than one fireplace. Tapestries, which are thick woven rugs, were often hung on the walls or used to cover windows to keep out drafts.

The bottom floor was at ground level. It was here where the vegetables and grains grown by the serfs were stored for the lord's family.

Outside there was a separate stable for the horses and a well to supply water to all the manor residents.

Draw a diagram of a manor house.

Life as a Serf

You wake up shivering on your prickly straw mattress and snuggle closer to your brother and sister to warm up. The wind is whistling through the cracks in the walls and the door. You hear your mother start a fire in the fire pit in the centre of the room. Soon, the fire crackles, and the small cottage begins to warm up. But the smoke makes your eyes sting. You yank the rough wool blanket away from your sister, and duck beneath it to hide from the smoke. In the stable on the other side of the wall, you hear your father tend to the animals.

The sun is not yet up when your mother calls for breakfast. The space on the bench where your youngest sister used to sit at meal times still looks so empty. She died of an infection before her second birthday, just like your twin brother did the year before. After morning prayers, you eat your share of porridge and a chunk of coarse homemade bread, and wash both down with a mug of ale.

It's time to do your chores. Everyone in the family has something to do. Today, you are working in the fields with your father and older brother. As you get ready, your mother and sister roll up the straw mattress you all sleep on. They will spend the morning sweeping the floor and cleaning and tidying up the cottage.

In the fields, your father works quickly. He rarely stops to talk. He is worried that the weeds will take over the crop of peas, and other crops may not be very good this year. That would mean little food next winter. You work extra hard so Father won't worry as much. You scare hundreds of blackbirds away from the newly sown field. The birds are eating the seed before it has a chance to grow! You also help Father pull out weeds. When the sun is halfway across the sky, your sister joins you to help. Back at the cottage, Mother dries peas in a pot of boiling water. She is cooking another pot of pease porridge.

When it is time for dinner, you all return to the cottage. Your mother has fetched water from the village well at the manor house. And she has fresh pease porridge waiting. There is bread and ale again and a small, hard piece of goat's cheese for everyone. Mother also lets you roast an apple on a stick over the fire. What a wonderful meal!

It is dark now. Father beds the animals down for the night while you help Mother unroll the big straw mattress. Everyone climbs into bed and snuggles up to keep warm on this cold and drafty night. Before you fall asleep, you say your prayers.

Serf's Cottage

The Home of a Serf

Serfs lived in a one-room or two-room cottage with a thatched roof. A thatched roof is made of bundles of reeds from riverbanks or layers of straw packed tightly together.

The cottage walls were made of something called *wattle and daub*. Wattle were twigs woven together, and daub was mud mixed with straw or horsehair. This was placed between the timber posts that made up the frame of the cottage.

The timber posts were cut from trees in the manor forest. The floor was bare earth. These cottages could be made quickly with materials found on the manor.

A round circle was marked in the centre of the cottage, and a fire pit was built there. Smoke from the fire found its way out of the cottage through a hole in the roof.

1. What is thatch, and what was it used for? _____

_____

_____

_____

2. What were the walls of the cottage made of? _____

_____

_____

_____

3. Do you think homes made of these materials would last a long time?

_____

_____

_____

_____

4. What problems might there be with a fire pit in a home with a thatch roof? _____

_____

_____

_____

5. Why do you think serfs built their homes using these materials? ____

_____

_____

_____

Name: _____

Date: _____

Comparing Medieval Society and Present-Day Life in Canada

Medieval Society

Present-Day Canada

1. _____

2. _____

3. _____

10 | Agricultural Methods

Background Information for Teachers

In this lesson, students will research and compare agricultural methods from medieval times and present day. Consider contacting your local agricultural office for brochures, posters, and other resources for this lesson.

Students will use a cooperative learning jigsaw method to learn about one farming process, and then share their findings with other groups.

Materials

- brochures and books on current agricultural methods in Canada
- reference books on medieval times
- medieval agriculture information sheets (included. Copy these sheets, and cut out cards.) (1.10.1)

Activity

As a class, discuss students' understanding of present-day agricultural methods. For example, ask:

- What kinds of machinery would you see on a farm today?
- How do farmers plough the fields?
- How do they fertilize land?
- How do they eliminate pests and weeds?

Record students' ideas, then compare agricultural methods during the Middle Ages. Ask:

- Would serfs have tools to help them do their farming?
- Have you observed any illustrations of farming methods during the Middle Ages?
- How would it have been different from today?

Divide the class into pairs, and provide each pair with one of the Medieval Agriculture

information sheets. Be sure to distribute the sheets so that groups are working on all topics. Have the students in each pair read their sheet and use the information to record ideas about their topic on the activity sheet (1.10.2).

Have students also examine resources related to current agricultural practices to answer the question presented on their information sheet, and to record these ideas on the activity sheet.

Once all pairs have completed their section of the activity sheet, group together two pairs of students that used different information sheets. Have the pairs share their findings with each other. This will provide an opportunity for them to complete another section of the activity sheet chart as they listen and glean ideas from their classmates.

Continue this process until all pairs have worked with other pairs on all topics, and until they have completed the activity sheet.

Activity Sheet

Directions to students:

Use the sheet to record information you find on agricultural methods in medieval times and present times. Record ideas using pictures and words (1.10.2).

Extensions

- Have local farmers visit the class as guest speakers to discuss how farming methods have changed over time.

- Visit local agricultural museums, many of which have displays of early farming tools similar to those used in medieval times.

Medieval Agriculture
Information Sheets

1. Preparing the Fields – Ploughing

In medieval times, farmers worked the field by hand. They were always inventing new methods to make their work easier or for growing more crops. One of the earliest tools used to prepare the soil was the *ard plough*. This lightweight plough, made of a horizontal wooden beam attached to an ard-head, cut the furrow or trench in the soil. An oxen, or horse, or even a farmer's wife was used to pull the plough!

Over time, *wheeled ploughs* were invented. These were heavier, but enabled farmers to break up hard, clay soil. These ploughs had one or two large wheels at the front that made it easier to steer and easier for animals to pull.

Farmers also began using horses more than ox, because horses were more versatile. They could be used for pulling ploughs and wagons, and they could be used for riding as well. However, there were problems with using horses for farming. Their hooves got soft in the damp soil, and cracked. Also, using the ox yoke to pull heavy loads cut off their breathing. Farmers found solutions to these problems. Nailed horseshoes were developed to help horses' hooves from injury during ploughing.

Also, padded horse collars began to be used, which made it easier for these strong animals to pull heavy loads without cutting into their windpipes.

How are fields prepared for planting on farms in Canada today?

What kinds of ploughs are used?

2. Seeding

Grains such as barley and oats were sown by hand, using a method called *broadcast sowing*. The farmer carried the seed in a large seed basket, called a *hopper*, and tossed the seed across the soil.

The seed then needed to be covered with soil. Farmers did this using a method called *harrowing*. One type of harrow consisted of a bundle of branches that was dragged over the land to spread the soil over the seeds. The harrow was pulled by a horse, sometimes even attached to its tail!

Another method of sowing seed was called *dibbling*. This was used for larger seeds, such as peas and beans. The farmer would use a poking stick called a *dibbler* or *dibble-stick* to make rows of small holes in the ground. The seeds were then dropped into the holes one at a time.

How are fields seeded on farms in Canada today?

3. Caring for the Soil

Fertilizer: The only form of fertilizer that medieval farmers had was animal *manure*. Farmers collected the manure to spread on fields, and animals were grazed on the fields after harvesting. Animals were also pastured in unplanted fields in order to fertilize the soil.

Ninth-century farmers began using a system called *three-crop rotation*. They divided their land into three fields, and planted two with crops in the spring and fall, while one field was left empty, or fallow. Leaving the field uncultivated and unplanted allowed it to replenish its nutrients. This chart shows the three-crop rotation system:

	Field 1	Field 2	Field 3
First Year	Fall – wheat and rye	Spring – oats, barley, peas, beans, lentils	Fallow
Second Year	Fallow	Fall – wheat and rye	Spring – oats, barley, peas, beans, lentils
Third Year	Spring – oats, barley, peas, beans, lentils	Fallow	Fall – wheat and rye

How are crops cared for on farms in Canada today?

What methods are used to fertilize soil?

Are crop rotations and fallow methods used today?

4. Caring for the Crops

Weeding: It was important for farmers to weed their fields so that the crops grew plentiful. This was done by hand with a small *sickle* and a stick with a Y-fork at the end. The stick was used to hold the weed, while the sickle was used to cut it off at the ground level.

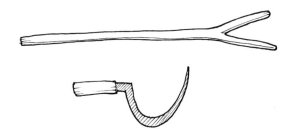

Keeping Pests Away: Birds often tried to eat newly sown seed, so children defended the fields from crows and other birds, using *slings* to hit the birds with rocks.

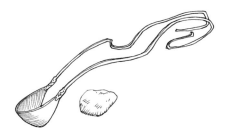

What methods are used for weed control on farms in Canada today?

What methods are used for pest control?

5. Harvesting

Haying: Haymaking was an important farming activity that provided winter *fodder*, or feed, for animals. Farmers used long-handled *scythes* to cut the hay close to the ground. Women and children followed behind the farmers, spreading out the hay so that it dried. The hay was then gathered into large stacks.

A *sickle* was the main tool used by medieval farmers to cut down wheat and corn. Wheat was cut down close to the ground, while corn was cut just below the ears. Sometimes poor peasants were allowed to *glean* whatever grain was left in the field before animals were released to graze on the stubble.

How are crops harvested on farms in Canada today?

How is haying done?

How are other crops removed from the fields?

6. Processing the Grain

To process the grain, a grainflail was used to thresh the grain from the plant. The grainflail was made from two pieces of wood tied together with a leather strip. The long handle was held as the beater hit against the grain.

Winnowing: After threshing, the grain was winnowed to remove straw and debris called *chaff*. This was done with a winnowing sheet, which was held and gently shaken by two or more people. Another method was to throw the grain up in the air over the winnowing sheet, which allowed the wind to blow away the lighter chaff and straw as the grain fell onto the sheet.

Sometimes winnowing fans were used for this task. With this method, the grain was scooped onto the fan and tossed gently in the air to sift out the chaff and straw.

How are crops processed in Canada today?

How is threshing done?

How is winnowing done?

Farming Methods

Process	Medieval Times	Present-Day Canada
Ploughing		
Seeding		
Caring for Crops (weeding, fertilizer, pest control)		
Harvesting		
Processing (threshing, winnowing)		

11 | Manor Law

Background Information for Teachers

Serfs had few rights on the manor. The manor lord decided their fate. If a serf was accused of a crime, physical punishments called *ordeals* were used to determine guilt or innocence. People believed God would save the innocent from the ordeals.

Materials

- chart paper
- markers
- play titled, "This Is the Law!" (included. Make a copy for each student.) (1.11.1)
- dictionaries
- writing paper
- reference books on medieval times

Activity: Part One: Canadian Law

Begin by discussing law in present-day society. Record the term *law* in the centre of a piece of chart paper. Create a concept web as discussion takes place. Ask:

- What does the term *law* mean? (look up the definition in the dictionary)
- What are some of the laws we have in our community?
- Who helps to enforce the law? (police, RCMP, judges)
- What happens in our community when someone is accused of a crime? (arrested, if there is evidence against him or her; trial with a jury and/or judge; a lawyer helps to defend the person)
- Have you ever heard the phrase "innocent until proven guilty"? What does it mean?

Provide students with a copy of the play, "This is the Law!" (included 1.11.1). Explain that this play is a fictional account showing how the legal system might work in Canada. Ask:

- What does fictional mean?

- Did this event really happen?

Provide students with a copy of Activity Sheet A (1.11.2). Have them read through the play independently, and complete the sheet to record the characters, events, and settings.

Divide the class into groups of 8 and have each group assign characters from the play. Have the groups read and rehearse the play, then perform it for one another.

Discuss the play, focusing on the legal issues that arose and the ways in which laws are enforced in Canada. Also, highlight what trials are like in Canada today.

Activity Sheet A

Directions to students:

Read the play, "This Is the Law," and record the characters, events, and setting on the story map. (1.11.2)

Activity: Part Two: Manor Law

Discuss the legal system in medieval time. Ask:

- What do you think happened to a serf if he was accused of a crime?
- What kinds of crimes might a serf be accused of?

Distribute activity sheet B (1.11.3) and read it together. Ask:

- Do you think these are fair ways to decide guilt or innocence?
- Do you think people who are accused of things are always guilty?

Have students complete the activity sheet.

Activity Sheet B

Directions to students:

Read the page again and answer the questions. Be sure to explain the reasons for your answers (1.11.3).

▶

11

Activity: Part Three: Re-creating Ordeals

Divide the class into working groups. Provide each group with activity sheet C (1.11.4). Challenge the groups to write a short play about a serf who has been accused of a crime. Have the groups use the activity sheet to plan their play, then write out the play in detail.

Note: Encourage the groups to use the play titled "This is the Law!" as a model to write their own play.

Provide plenty of time for the groups to write their plays, practice, and even make costumes. When all groups have finished, invite them to share their plays with the class. Discuss the plays, the crimes, the ordeals, and how the students felt about the situations presented.

Activity Sheet C

Directions to students:

Use the activity sheet to plan your play, then write the play out. In your groups, identify who will play each part, practice your play, and present it to the class (1.11.4).

Assessment Suggestion

Have students complete the student self-assessment sheet on page 19 to reflect on their ideas about manor law.

This Is the Law!

Scene One – Rural gas station. (Attendant is behind the counter, talking on the telephone.)

Attendant: (on phone) Well, okay then, I'll buy a newspaper when I drop off the recycling at the depot. Talk to you la….

Robber: (storms through the door) Hey, get off that phone, and hand over the cash, right now!

Attendant: BBBut….

Robber: I said now!

Attendant: Okay, okay, give me a minute here. I have to open the cash register.

Robber: Hurry up!

Attendant: (fiddling with the register, fumbling with the keys) I'm trying…

Robber: I haven't got all day here, ya' know. For the last time, hurry up!

Attendant: The key won't work. Hold on, I'll try the other set of keys.

Robber: Oh, brother, what a joke! Move it!

Attendant: (fumbling in drawer behind counter)

OPP Officer: (barges through the door, gun held up) Hold it right there. Hands up!
(OPP Officer handcuffs the robber) You're off to jail, buddy, then off to court!
(Officer drags robber out)

Scene Two – Court room (Robber sitting at one table with his defence lawyer. Prosecutor at other table, with gas station attendant and OPP Officer sitting behind her.)

Court Clerk: All rise for Judge Razam.
(everyone in the court stands as the judge enters and sits down)
Please be seated.

Judge: Mr. Jeffrey James, you are here today charged with attempted robbery. How do you plead?

Defence Lawyer: (Robber and his lawyer stand up) Your Honour, my client acknowledges his wrongdoing and pleads guilty, but begs the courts compassion in passing sentence.

Judge: Guilty plea is recorded, which means I will now consider sentencing. First, however, does the defendant wish to speak?

Robber: (stands) I do, Your Honour.

Judge: Then now is your chance.

Robber: Your Honour, I know that I tried to steal money from that gas station, and I know it was wrong. I have never been in trouble with the law before, but I was desperate. I lost my job and I had no money. I promise, if you let me go, I'll never be back here again.

Judge: Is that all?

Robber: I'm very sorry for what I did.

Judge: Does the prosecution have anything to add?

Prosecutor: Yes, Your Honour, we do. This man may sound regretful now, but he terrorized this gas station attendant, who is now too afraid to go to work and can't sleep at night. How is he supposed to care for his family? We're all just lucky that the OPP Officer came along, or that family may have lost its husband and father!

Defence Lawyer: Objection, Your Honour! My client had no weapon. This was an act of desperation. He wasn't thinking straight.

Judge: Objection sustained. You are correct, he had no weapon. However, he did indeed leave a victim in this case. A man too afraid to work or sleep is still a victim even though he may not have been physically harmed. Anything else from the prosecution?

Prosecutor: Yes, Your Honour. We request a prison sentence, even though this is a first offense. As I said, there was a victim here.

Judge: No doubt, there are always victims when a crime has been committed. I am ready to present my decision. Jeffrey James, please stand.

(robber and defence lawyer stand)

Judge: In this case, we have a first-time offender who has shown remorse, but who still, in fact, broke the law. I am sentencing you to three months incarceration, but I will suspend that sentence in light of your clean past record and I also sentence you to 200 hours of community work, in the community where the crime took place. I will also require you to participate in employment counselling in order to find another job and stay out of trouble. Take this as a warning, and as a second chance. If you end up back in court again, no one will be lenient. Do you understand, Mr. James?

Robber: Yes, sir, thank you, sir.

Judge: Baliff, Mr. James is free to go. All adjourned.

Court Clerk: All rise.

(everyone stands as the judge leaves)

THE END

Name: _____

Story Map for a Play

"This is the Law"

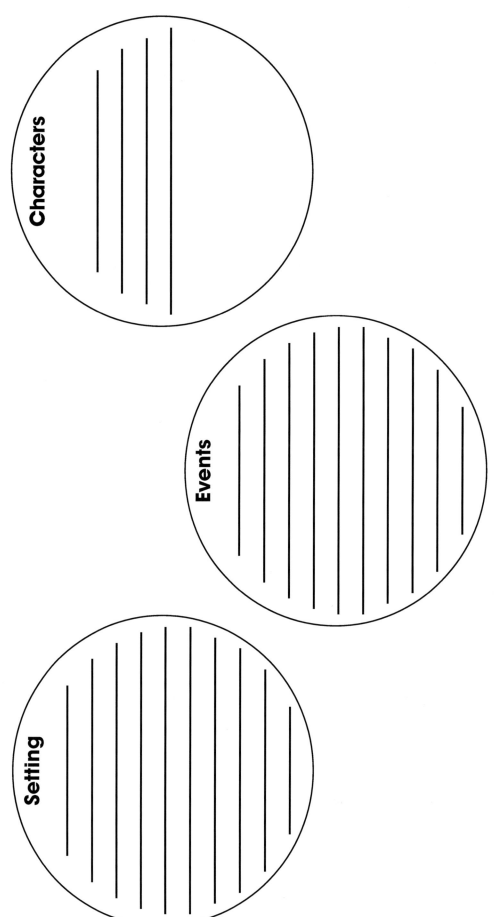

Characters

Events

Setting

Manor Law

For most people in medieval times, the lord of the manor was the law. He represented the king in all local matters. Serfs were not free and, therefore, not entitled to a trial to decide their guilt or innocence. Instead, the lord decided their fate when they were accused of a crime. Often this fate was decided by an ordeal. People believed that God would help the innocent in these ordeals. Three types of ordeals were used:

Ordeal by fire: The accused placed a hand in boiling water or carried a red hot metal bar a specified distance. If the wound from the burn healed within a certain time period, the accused was innocent. If not, the accused was found guilty and punished.

Ordeal by water: The accused was tied and thrown in water. If the accused floated he or she was guilty. If the accused sank, he or she was innocent, but needed to be rescued quickly!

Ordeal by fighting: If two people were accusing each other, they would be ordered to fight. The winner was declared innocent, and the loser was declared guilty.

1. Do you think the ordeals used were a fair way to decide if a person was innocent or guilty? Why or why not?

   _____

   _____

   _____

2. What happens to a person who is accused of a crime today in our community?

   _____

   _____

   _____

Date: _____

Planning a Play

Ordeal By _____

Name: _____

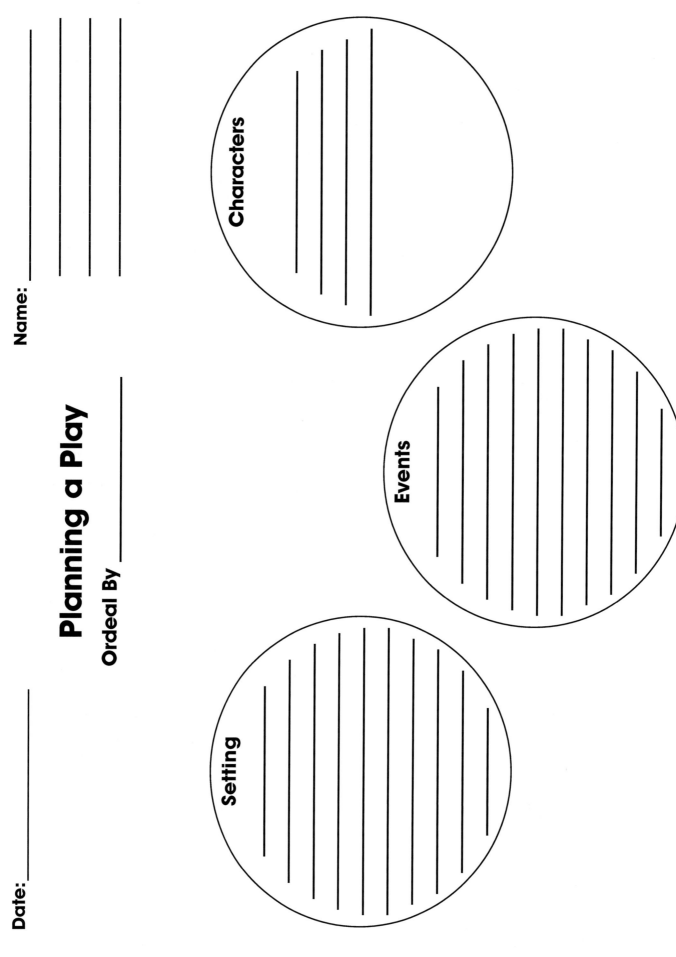

Characters

Events

Setting

12 | Jobs in a Medieval Town

Background Information for Teachers

Most people in medieval society had to work on farms to ensure there would be enough food for everyone. Early in the eleventh century, a new type of plough was invented that produced better crop yields. This meant that fewer people were needed to work the land, and people could specialize in other trades.

Towns developed on manor land around castles. The manor lord still controlled the land on which towns were built, so the townspeople paid rent in return for their freedom.

Soon, people began to make a living at such trades as carpentry and blacksmithing. When groups of craftsmen decided to establish rules and standards for their trade, the first guilds were formed. Guilds were similar to today's unions – they controlled prices and decided how apprentices should be trained. Both boys and girls could be apprentices. Members from the same guild often had their shops all on one street. Since most people could not read, each guild had a symbol for its craft. These symbols were displayed in front of their workshops.

Materials

- *Mathilda Bone*, by Karen Cushman
- chart paper
- markers
- reference books about life in medieval towns
- index cards
- coloured pencils

Activity: Part One: Skilled Craftspeople

Begin by reviewing life on the manor. Ask:

- How did the serfs make a living on the manor?
- What kinds of crops did they grow?
- Could they keep any of their crops?

Explain that, over time, people learned better ways to farm and invented new ploughs. They were able to produce better and bigger crops. Soon they were selling extra crops to make money. With better equipment, fewer people were needed to work the land. Some bought their freedom from the manor lord and moved away from the serfs' cottages. Villages and towns grew, and people learned new skills to make a living in the towns. People who made goods and sold them were called *craftsmen*. Ask:

- What types of things can you buy today in shops and stores?

Record a list of things we buy. Discuss which things students think could be bought in medieval towns and which could not. Circle the things that were likely available back then.

Now provide students with reference books about medieval towns. Have them identify craftsmen who made and sold goods. Record students' suggestions on chart paper. (Some of the jobs done in castles were also done by town craftsmen, so students may remember some of these jobs from previous lessons.) Possible suggestions include:

Potter: dishes and ornaments
Cobbler: shoes and boots
Blacksmith: nails, iron cart tires, tools
Brewster or **Brewer**: beer and ale
Glassblower: glass dishes, ornaments, and bottles
Stone carver: statues
Carpenter: furniture, house frames
Baker: bread and pastries
Tapestry maker: carpets
Goldsmith: jewellery
Weaver: fabric for clothes

Have students focus on how people trained to become craftsmen. Ask:

- How do people learn job skills today? (school, university, technical colleges, on-the-job training)
- How do you think people in medieval times learned to be skilled craftsmen?
- Do you think there were many colleges and universities back then?

Distribute the activity sheet, and read the text together. Discuss the ways that craftsmen learned their trades and formed guilds. Then have the students design symbols for each trade listed.

Following completion of the activity sheet, have each student select a symbol and draw it on an index card. Display the cards and have other students guess the craft that is represented by each symbol.

Activity Sheet

Directions to students:

Read the information, then select a medieval trade that you would like to make a guild symbol for. Draw this symbol on the sheet. Next draw a symbol to represent each trade listed on your sheet. Choose one symbol and redraw it on an index card. Ask your classmates if they can guess which guild your symbol is for (1.12.1).

Activity: Part Two

Read *Matilda Bone*, by Karen Cushman. This book is full of rich descriptions of the harsh life in a town, and the struggle of a young peasant girl to survive in medieval times as she learns a trade.

Activity: Part Three

Family Names: As town populations grew, people needed a better way to refer to each other than by first name alone. They began to use surnames as a way of identifying people with the same first name. There were different

ways English surnames were chosen. For example:

- **occupation**: Archer, Baker, Cooper
- **physical appearance**: Black, Armstrong, Small
- **place**: Dale, Rivers, Forest
- **town or village**: London, Lancaster, Cornwall
- **family relations**: Johnson, Thomson, Richardson (son of Richard)
- **title**: Bishop, Knight, Lord, Freeman

Have students research their own family names. (Other cultures may have similar origins for names.) Students should interview family members or check the Internet for information on names. Have students print their surname on a card along with an explanation for the origin of their name. Prepare a bulletin board display titled "What's in a Name?" and place name cards with origins on the board for all to see.

Activity Centre

Focus on a particular type of skill or craft, such as stone carving, and present information about the skill and pictures of actual crafts that date from medieval times. For example, stone carvers made gargoyles, which were placed on the great cathedrals being built. The gargoyles provided a downspout to drain the water away from the stone of the church walls. There are many interesting books about gargoyles and many calendars that feature gargoyles from this time. Have pictures of gargoyles available at the centre. Encourage students to draw gargoyles and write poetry describing the emotions evident on the faces, or what gargoyles would say if they could talk.

Note: The Parliament Buildings in Ottawa have many interesting gargoyles. You may wish to collect pictures of these so students can compare and contrast them with medieval gargoyles.

Becoming a Skilled Craftsman

Apprentices

People started to learn their trade when they were children. Both boys and girls were sent by their family to live and work with a master craftsman. This training was called an *apprenticeship*. For the first while, apprentices spent most of their time doing chores to make the master's life easier. In a way, the apprentice was a servant. However, the master craftsman had to make sure apprentices were taught the skills of the trade and would be ready to work on their own after seven years. These rules were decided upon by a group of craftsmen in the same trade. This group was called a *guild*.

Guilds

Guilds were unions, or groups, of people who worked in the same trade. The guild decided how apprentices should be trained and controlled prices of items sold by guild members. The guild made sure everyone's work was of good quality.

Since most people in medieval times could not read or write, guild members put picture signs above their stalls or shops so that people would know what was sold there. Each guild had one sign that was used by all its members to show that they belonged to that guild. A guild of cobblers, for example, used a picture of a boot as their symbol.

1. Select a medieval trade and draw a symbol for it.

Trade _____

2. Can you think of some symbols that might have been used to represent these guilds? Draw a symbol for each.

Fishmonger   **Baker**

Carpenter   **Blacksmith**

13 The Plague

Background Information for Teachers

Towns were not kept very clean; people did not know how to properly dispose of garbage and sewage. Garbage and chamber pot contents, for example, were thrown out the upper windows into the gutter. These practices produced ideal conditions for the spread of disease; rats and other animals thrived in the lanes and gutters as they rooted through the garbage. The Black Death, which swept through Europe from 1347–1349, killed about 1/4–1/3 of the population. It was due, indirectly, to the unsanitary living conditions. The disease was carried by rats. It passed into the human population when fleas carrying infected blood from the rodents bit people.

Materials

- green construction paper
- Lego or building blocks
- small Post-it Notes
- picture titled, "Medieval Town" (included. Make an overhead transparency of this sheet.) (1.13.1)
- overhead projector
- chart paper
- markers
- dictionaries
- poster board

Activity: Part One: Medieval Towns

Begin by discussing the use of stone walls for castles and manor houses. Ask:

- Why were walls built around castles and manor houses?
- What were the walls made of?
- How did the walls protect the people inside them?

Explain that towns, as well, were built within walls to protect the inhabitants from enemy attacks.

Divide the class into working groups, and provide each group with a piece of green construction paper, black markers, blocks, and Post-it Notes. Explain that the green sheet represents the land within the town walls. Have the groups draw a thick black line around the edge of their paper to represent the walls of the town. Ask:

- What do you think would be in the town?
- What kinds of buildings would be in the town?

As students suggest buildings such as houses and shops, have them use blocks to represent the buildings and place them inside the town walls. Discuss the types of shops that would be in the town, and add several buildings within the walls. Students can use Post-it Notes to label the buildings. Ask:

- What do you think happened as more people moved to the town? (add more buildings)
- What happened when there was no more land left to build buildings on?

Explain that the towns became very crowded and that people built second, third, and fourth floors onto existing buildings. Have the groups add blocks on top of the existing ones to represent this expansion.

Discuss the crowding of the town as more people arrived and buildings expanded. Explain that eventually the town grew beyond the walls. Display the diagram of the medieval town (1.13.1). Discuss the diagram, focusing on the buildings and features of the town.

Distribute activity sheet A (1.13.2). In their groups, have the students read, discuss, and respond to the questions.

▶

13

As a class, discuss the groups' responses to the questions on the activity sheet. Explain that because there was no way to get rid of sewage and garbage, they were simply thrown into the streets. Discuss what it would have been like to live in these conditions and some of the problems that might have occurred.

Activity Sheet A

Note: This is a two-page activity sheet.

Directions to students:

In your group, read each question and record your answers (1.13.2).

Activity: Part Two: The Plague

Compare the pollution problems of medieval towns with those in our towns and cities today. Title a sheet of chart paper *Pollution Problems.* Divide the sheet into two columns: *Medieval Town* and *Our Community Today*. Have students discuss the pollution problems of both time periods. An interesting parallel might be between the poor water quality in medieval towns and recent water pollution problems in some communities in Ontario.

Discuss health concerns related to pollution. Ask:

- What do you think happens to people living in polluted areas?
- What might happen if they drink polluted water?
- What might happen if garbage is left to rot everywhere?

Hand out activity sheet B (1.13.3) and read it together. Discuss the causes for the Black Death (also called the Plague) in Europe and what it might have been like to live then. Have the students use their dictionaries to complete the activity sheet.

Activity Sheet B

Directions to students:

Read this page again. Use a dictionary to find the correct definitions for each word. Sometimes there is more than one meaning for a word. How do you decide which is the meaning you want? (Look for a meaning that has to do with sickness, since that is the topic of the information sheet.) Answer the question at the bottom of the page (1.13.3).

Activity: Part Three

Discuss health and environmental issues as they relate to the Plague. Ask:

- What caused the Plague?
- Could the Plague have been avoided? How?
- What recommendations would you make that might have helped save lives during this time?

Brainstorm ideas and record students' suggestions. Have each student design a poster that might have been helpful in educating the public during medieval times. The poster should focus on health, hygiene, sanitation, or environmental concerns of this time.

Extensions

- Have the students create a three-dimensional model of a medieval town. Students can draw blueprints, using the extension activity sheet (1.13.4). On the sheet, they can draw a map of houses, shops, the town church, and other buildings they have noticed in pictures of medieval towns. They should also include a legend so that they can identify the

13

buildings. Students can then use a board as the base for the land, build a wall from blocks or Lego, and construct buildings from boxes and blocks.

- In North America, Quebec City is the only example of a walled city. Collect pictures and photographs of "Old Quebec" City and have students compare and contrast the city with medieval walled towns.

- Translations of first-hand accounts of the Plague can be found on the Internet (see Web Sites). You may wish to read one of these aloud to impress upon the students the horror of this widespread epidemic and the importance of living in sanitary conditions.

- Take a field trip to the landfill site in your community, or show videos of the pollution problems we face today. Compare problems today to the types of pollution problems medieval communities faced.

- Have students investigate epidemics that have occurred in Canada or in their own community and how long ago these epidemics occurred.

- Invite a public health nurse to talk to the class about the importance of hygiene.

- Take a tour of a water treatment plant. Observe the many steps necessary to make sure the water supply is clean. Compare this water source with the water supply in medieval towns. In medieval society, why do you think everyone preferred to drink ale rather than water?

Medieval Town

Date:_____   Name: _____

_____

_____

_____

Medieval Towns

1. **Medieval towns were built within stone walls. Why do you think there were walls around the towns?** _____

_____

_____

_____

_____

2. **The walls meant that there was only a limited amount of room in the town. Most buildings were built very close together to save space. They were made of wood frames with plaster or of wattle and daub walls. What other buildings were made of wattle and daub?** _____

_____

_____

_____

_____

3. **With little room to sprawl within the town walls, buildings were built up two or three floors when more room was needed. The upper floors jutted out over the streets. Why did townspeople try to be careful with fires?** _____

_____

_____

_____

_____

4. **There was no running water or drains of any kind in the towns. What sort of problems do you think this caused?** _____

_____

_____

_____

_____

5. **There were no toilets or cesspits like in the castle. Where do you think these wastes were put?** _____

_____

_____

_____

_____

6. **There were no sanitation workers to pick up trash outside the homes. Where do you think the garbage went?** _____

_____

_____

_____

_____

7. **Describe what you think life was like in a medieval town.**

_____

_____

_____

_____

_____

The Plague

With all the garbage and sewage in the streets, towns soon were full of rats and other animals that eat garbage. The unclean conditions provided an ideal environment for the spread of many diseases. During the Middle Ages, the Black Death was the worst disease of all. From 1347 to 1349, almost a third of the population of Europe died from the Black Death. In some villages, there were not enough people alive to bury the dead.

Many people believed the Black Death epidemic was God's way of punishing them. Some gave up all physical comforts and carried signs asking God to forgive their sins and spare them from the plague. They did not know that this disease, also called bubonic or pneumonic plague, was caused by bacteria. Nor did they know that the rats roaming the towns and cities were covered in fleas that carried the bacteria. When the fleas bit people, they passed the bacteria on to humans.

Several other diseases were spread by body lice and fleas on animals and people – typhus, cholera, smallpox, and influenza, to name a few.

Use a dictionary to find and define the meaning of these words:

plague: _____

epidemic: _____

disease: _____

bacteria: _____

Why are we safe from most epidemics today? _____

_____

_____

Name: _____

Date: _____

Blueprint for a Medieval Town

Legend

14 Religion

Background Information for Teachers

This lesson serves as an introduction to some of the religions that influenced life in the Middle Ages. It is important to consider students' religious beliefs and backgrounds when dealing with religious issues, especially in multicultural classrooms. At the same time, this serves and an excellent opportunity to help develop a better understanding of different belief systems, and to respect this type of diversity in the classroom, and in society.

Materials

- information sheets on Judaism, Christianity, and Islam (included. Make copies for each student. (1.14.1)
- chart paper
- markers
- 3 chart-sized copies of activity sheet A (1.14.2)
- highlighters (or coloured pens/pencils)
- reference books on places of worship during medieval times
- digital camera

Activity: Part One

Provide students with the information sheet (1.14.1) on Judaism. Allow them time to read through the sheet silently. Ask:

- What religion is described on this sheet?
- How did this religion begin?
- What are the main beliefs in this religion?
- What is the holy book called?
- What celebrations are described?

Have students highlight words and phrases as they find the answers to these questions, and discuss the information presented.

Using a chart-sized copy of the activity sheet (1.14.2), model how to complete this three-

point-approach chart, using ideas and answers provided during the discussion.

Now divide the class into pairs, and provide each pair with a copy of the activity sheet. Give half the groups the information sheet on Christianity and half the information sheet on Islam. Have the students complete the three-point-approach chart for this religion.

Once all groups have completed this task, have them share their results with the class. As they do, record their findings on the chart-sized three-point-approach charts.

Activity Sheet

Directions to students:

Use the ideas on the information sheet to complete the chart. Use both words and illustrations to complete the chart. (1.14.2)

Activity: Part Two

Examine buildings in your local community that are the centres of worship for these three religious faiths. Go on a community walk or bus ride to take photos of churches, mosques, and synagogues.

Have students examine reference books and web sites to examine places of worship from the Middle Ages. Collect illustrations and photos of these as well.

Compare the buildings from past and present times, and discuss features of each place of worship.

Display the various pictures with the large three-point-approach charts completed in Activity: Part One.

Judaism

Judaism is the parent faith of Christianity. It began in the Middle East over 4000 years ago, and was founded by Moses and Abraham. Jews believe that there is only one god who created and rules the world. Moses is believed to be the greatest prophet in the Jewish faith. He was given the Torah, which is the Jewish holy book. He also received the Ten Commandments from God at Mount Sinai, and the Israelites with him committed themselves to following this code of how people practice their faith and treat one another. The Ten Commandments are:

1. I am the Lord your God.

2. You shall not recognize other gods.

3. You shall not take the Name of your Lord in vain.

4. Remember the day of Shabbat and keep it holy.

5. Honour your father and your mother.

6. You shall not murder.

7. You shall not commit adultery.

8. You shall not steal.

9. You shall not give false testimony against your neighbour.

10. You shall not covet your fellow's possessions.

Passover is a Jewish celebration in April. It commemorates the birth of the Jewish nation and the freedom of the Jews. After 210 years of slavery in Egypt, Moses told Pharoah, "Let my people go." It is believed that God brought a plague upon the Egyptians. The 10th and final plague was the death of first-born children. But God "passed over" Jewish homes, hence the name of the celebration, Passover.

Christianity

Christianity originally developed as a part of Judaism. Jesus Christ was a Jew. He lived from about 3 BCE to 30 CE. He lived and taught in Palestine, among fellow Jews. Christians separated from the Jews because they came to regard Jesus as God's presence in human form. Christmas, which celebrates Jesus' birth, is an important time in Christian faith.

Christians believe in one God, who created the universe. They see human beings as created in the image of God. Christians also follow The Ten Commandments, and the teachings of the Holy Bible. They also believe that Jesus, born of the Virgin Mary, was crucified on the cross, but rose again to heaven to sit by God's side. Easter celebrates the day of Jesus' resurrection, and is an important Christian holiday. Christians also believe that Jesus's resurrection showed them that they can also resurrect to heaven after death.

There are many different denominations, or faith groups, within Christianity. Catholic, Anglican, United, Baptist, Mormon, and Mennonite are just a few. There are also many non-denominational Christian churches, as well as evangelical and fellowship groups.

Islam

During the Middle Ages, Christianity grew in western Europe, but the religion of Islam developed in other parts of the world. Islam is based on the teachings of the prophet, Muhammad, and the people who follow this religion are called *Muslims*. Muhammad was born around 570 CE, at a time when Arabs were worshipping many different spirits. According to Muhammad, he was visited by an angel named Gabriel, who told him that there was only one god. Muslims call God *Allah*.

Muslims follow their Islamic faith through The Five Pillars, which are duties that all believers must follow:

Shahadah – to declare belief in one God and Muhammad as God's messenger

Salah – to pray five times a day

Sawm – to fast during the month of Ramadan

Zakah – to donate 2.5% of earning each year to those less fortunate

Hajj – to make a pilgrimage to the city of Mecca

Ramadan is an Islamic celebration that takes place in the 9th month of the Muslim calendar, in November, December, January, or February (depending on the sighting of the moon). For a whole month, Muslims fast during the day. It is a time for worship, and a time to strengthen family and community ties.

For a fifth of the world's population, Islam is both a religion and a complete way of life.

Date: _____   Name: _____

Three-Point Approach

History	Religion	Beliefs
	Celebrations	

15 The Roman Church

Background Information for Teachers

The church of medieval Europe was the Roman Catholic church. It played such an important role in society that medieval Europe was known as Christendom to its inhabitants.

The head of the Church was the pope in Rome. The Church followed a hierarchy:

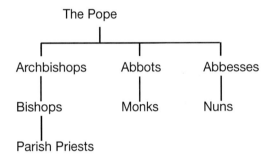

The pope, archbishops, abbots, abbesses, and bishops were all from noble families. Abbesses were often noblewomen who chose the church rather than marriage. They were not necessarily religious. Some, in fact, had very little faith and just wanted power and independence. For women in the Middle Ages, the church was the only way to attain this.

Parish priests were often from peasant families, and monks and nuns could be from any class. Through the Church, a person of low birth could receive an education and rise to fill a position of importance in the Church, monastery, or convent.

The Church owned a great deal of land – many noblemen left land to the Church when they died. Abbeys were large estates, consisting of many buildings including either a monastery under the supervision of an abbot, or a convent under the supervision of an abbess.

Monasteries and convents were the centres of learning in medieval times. Monks educated the children of nobility (although minimally),

copied books by hand and illustrated them (called *illuminated manuscripts*), cared for the sick, provided shelter for travellers, recorded important events that occurred, and provided a stabilizing influence on society by following the Church rules.

Materials

- information sheet titled, "The Church" (included. Make a copy for each student.) (1.15.2)
- overhead diagram of medieval town (from lesson 13)
- picture titled, "Medieval Church" (included. Make an overhead transparency of this sheet.) (1.15.1)
- overhead projector
- colour prints from illuminated manuscript pages (These are available on the Internet at www.image.ox.ac.uk/)
- white squares of poster board (one for each student)
- pencils
- assorted markers, glitter pens, or paints and paintbrushes
- chart paper

Activity: Part One: The Medieval Church

Display the overhead of the medieval town (from lesson 13). Discuss the features of the town, and ask:

- Can you locate the church in this town?
- How do you know it is a church?
- What characteristics do churches have?
- How is the church different from other buildings in the town?

Now display the overhead of the medieval church (1.15.1). Discuss the size and grandeur of the cathedral as a marked contrast to the humble buildings of the common people. Ask:

▶

15

- Do you think this church was easy to build? Why or why not?
- Why do you think people of medieval times put so much effort and expense into constructing these buildings?

Distribute the information sheet (1.15.2), and read it to the class. As you read, have students use activity sheet A (1.15.3) to take notes about the information presented. Discuss the role of the Church. Ask:

- What did the Church provide for people in medieval times?

Record students' suggestions on chart paper.

Activity Sheet A

Directions to students:

As the information sheet is read, take notes on what you hear about the Church in medieval times (1.15.3).

Activity: Part Two: Illuminated Manuscripts

Display examples of illuminated manuscript pages, and provide students with activity sheet B (1.15.4). Read the text together while referring to the examples displayed. Discuss the patterns, colours, and types of pictures that were used. Encourage students to experiment with this technique, with the letter A on the bottom of the activity sheet.

Now challenge the students to make an illuminated manuscript of their first name. Provide them with poster board and pencils. Students should sketch their name and design first with pencil. Encourage them to illustrate to the edges of the card as in the examples. Suggest they include things that are important to them in their illustrations, such as hobbies, physical traits, skills, and interests. When they have completed their pencil sketches, have

students add colour with markers, glitter pens, and paints. These name "manuscripts" can be displayed in the classroom. Challenge the students to identify the significance of the symbols in the designs used by others.

Activity Sheet B

Directions to students:

After reading about how nuns and monks created illuminated manuscripts, try this technique with the letter A. Now make an illuminated manuscript of your first name (1.15.4).

Extensions

- Examine pictures of medieval churches, cathedrals, monasteries, and convents, and discuss the features of these structures. (There are many Internet sites that offer pictures of these buildings. See Web Sites.)

- Encourage students to read about the workday of monks and nuns. A report could be presented to the rest of the class. Students could debate if it would be better to be a noblewoman, a serf, or a nun, and explain why.

- Research pilgrimages. During medieval times, many people travelled on foot, horseback, or by boat to visit the tombs of saints. The remains of these saints were kept in special tombs in many cathedrals and churches. The people believed that if they visited these tombs, they would receive blessings or, if they were sick, become healed. Geoffrey Chaucer was a poet who wrote about a pilgrimage in a poem called *The Canterbury Tales*. Using the extension activity sheet (1.15.5), challenge students to translate part of this poem into modern English.

Medieval Church

The Church

The Church was very important to the people of medieval Europe. Most Europeans were Christians and belonged to what we call the Roman Catholic Church. Everyone had to give one tenth of their money, goods, or crops to the Church. They believed that if they went to church, prayed, and followed the Church rules, they would go to heaven when they died. They lived hard lives and hoped for a better life in heaven.

Each town had a priest who was the head of the Church. The priest was given land from the manor. He was paid for performing weddings, baptisms, and burials. The serfs farmed the land for their priest. People believed that they could speak to God through their priest.

Monks and nuns played important roles in the Church. They were taught to read and write. Some learned the skills needed to be an artist, practice medicine (as it was known then), compose and play music, or teach noble children the basics of reading and writing. Here are some of the jobs undertaken by monks and nuns:

- **Care for the Sick:** Monks kept infirmaries, which were a type of hospital. They used herbs from their gardens to make medicines. Nuns also ran hospitals to care for the sick.

- **Shelter for Travellers:** Monks provided rooms and food for travellers.

- **Skilled Farmers:** Like the manor serfs, monks grew their own foods. They had many fields and orchards, and they were skilled at growing a variety of crops. They also made wine and cheese.

- **Recorded Important Events:** Much of the information we have today about medieval life comes from the records that were kept by monks. Since most of the people of this time could not read or write, recording events was an important job.

Date:_____   Name: _____

The Medieval Church

Note-Taking

The Church	

The Priest	

Monks and Nuns	

Book Makers

One very important job performed by monks and nuns was copying and translating books. There were no printing presses in the Middle Ages, and making a book took a year or more. Each book was printed out by hand, using a quill pen. There was no paper; book pages were made from sheepskin known as *vellum*. It could take a lot of sheep to make one book! Books were often decorated with patterns and pictures around the edges of the text. This was called *illuminated manuscript*.

Usually, a scribe would print the words on the page and an illuminator – a type of artist – would paint the colourful illustrations around the edges of the page.

Look at some samples of illuminated manuscripts. Try the same techniques on the letter A. You can see that decorating books was a time-consuming job! If ink spilled on the vellum, or a mistake was made, the illuminator had to start the page all over again.

Letter *A*:

Medieval Poetry

Here is part of *The Canterbury Tales* by the English poet, Geoffrey Chaucer (c. 1340-1400). His poem is about a group of people going on a pilgrimage. Who do you think he is describing in this section of the poem:

A knyght ther was, and that a worthy man,

That fro the tyme that he first bigan

To riden out, he loved chivalrie,

Trouthe and honour, fredom and curteisie.

Ful worthy was he in his lordes werre,

And therto hadde he riden, no man ferre,

As wel in cristendom as in hethenesse,

And evere honoured for his worthynesse.

Can you tell what Chaucer is saying? When Chaucer wrote this poem, people spoke what we now call "middle English" – a form of English different from the one we speak today. Try to translate each line into modern English.

_____

_____

_____

_____

_____

_____

16 | The Crusades

Background Information for Teachers

In the eleventh century, Pope Urban II called upon all Christian knights to wage war against the Muslims. Each year, many Christian Europeans made the pilgrimage to Jerusalem, and Muslims were now preventing them from entering the city. In the ensuing war, the Christians won Jerusalem back. About fifty years later, the two sides were again at war. This time, the Christians lost Jerusalem to the Muslims and never won it back again. These wars are called *Crusades* and are often referred to as *Holy Wars,* because they took place in the Holy Land between Christians and Muslims. Five major Crusades took place over a 200-year period, and many thousands of lives were lost on each side.

Knights who had no inheritance were among those most eager to fight in the Crusades. England was not the only country to fight; all of Christendom took part, including France, as well as Italian and German states.

Before the Crusades, medieval Europe, or Christendom, was relatively isolated. Although some trading occurred, trade with countries to the east did not open up until after the Crusades. Then, many products and ideas were introduced to Europe. These included foods such as almonds, black pepper, cloves, dates, figs, ginger, lemons, nutmeg, oranges, raisins, rice, and sugar; items like carpets, enamel, forks, glass, jewellery, mattresses, mirrors, muslin (cotton), perfume, satin, silk, sofas, and soap; concepts and ideas such as Arabic numerals, medical knowledge, and scientific knowledge.

New words from the Islamic countries included *admiral, algebra, almanac, azure, bazaar, caravan, cipher, elixir, jar,* and *julep*.

During the Crusades, most Christians were Europeans and most Muslims were Arabs.

Materials

- chart paper
- markers
- information sheet titled, "The Crusades" (included. Make a copy for each student.) (1.16.1)
- map of medieval Europe and the Holy Land, now called the Middle East, from lesson 3 (Make an overhead of this sheet. Have students use their copy from lesson 3.)
- overhead projector
- samples of items from the Holy Land that were brought back to Europe after the Crusades (e.g., bar of soap, almonds, playing cards (with Arabic numerals), black pepper, assorted whole spices, lemon, orange, raisins, perfume, rice, sugar. Place them in a bag.)

Activity: Part One: The Crusades

Review what students have learned about the Church; refer to the sheet that reflected ways the Church helped people of the Middle Ages (see page 124). Review how rich and powerful the Church was and how people believed they would not go to heaven if they did not follow church laws.

Explain that during the Middle Ages many Christians made trips to Jerusalem. They considered Jerusalem to be in the Holy Land because that is where Jesus was born. These trips were called *pilgrimages*. Record this term on chart paper.

16

Display the map of medieval Europe and the Holy Land on the overhead projector, and identify Jerusalem. Have students mark Jerusalem on their copy of the map.

Distribute the information sheet about the Crusades (1.16.1), and read it together.

Discuss the Crusades, focusing on what they were and why they happened. Explain that during medieval times Christians believed that anyone who was not a Christian was a "heathen" – someone who would not go to heaven. Christians believed they were doing God's will when they fought the Muslims. Ask:

- What do you think the Muslims thought?

Explain that Muslims also believe in God. They follow the teachings of Muhammad, a prophet of God. Ask:

- Do you think the pope should have called for a Holy War?
- Can you think of any other solutions that could have been tried?

Following this discussion, have students complete activity sheet A (1.16.1).

Activity Sheet A

Directions to students:

Read the information sheet again (1.16.1). Use the words at the top of the page to complete the sentences about the Crusades (1.16.2).

Activity: Part Two: Trade with People of the Holy Land

Review the reasons that the Crusades occurred, and discuss the effects of these Holy Wars on the people. Ask:

- How do wars affect people?
- What is the worst thing about war?
- Were there any good things that happened because of the Crusades?

Remind the students that although many people died in the Holy Wars, the Crusades resulted in the people in these two regions learning more about each other. They started trading goods and sharing ideas.

Now display the bag of items. Explain that the items in this bag are just some of the goods that people in medieval Europe were introduced to, or learned about, from the Muslims. Before the Crusades, none of these items was known in Europe.

Remove the objects from the bag one at a time, and pass them around. Challenge the students to explain why these items would be important to people in medieval Europe (e.g., soap resulted in better sanitary conditions and hygiene; spices added flavour to food and helped to hide the taste of rancid meat).

Allow the students to examine the items as they complete activity sheet B (1.16.3).

Activity Sheet B

Directions to students:

Draw a variety of items that Islamic countries introduced to Europe. Label the items, and explain what they might be used for (1.16.3).

Activity: Part Three: Other Influences From the East

The Islamic people significantly influenced life in medieval Europe. They contributed to this society in a variety of ways beyond traded goods. Have students research and present on contributions such as:

- Islamic architecture and its influence on medieval castles
- Islamic medicine, and the works of Avicenna, who wrote *The Canon of Medicine*, a reference book used by doctors in Europe into the 17th century.

16

- Al-Razi, who developed vaccinations for diseases such as small pox
- Arabic number system
- Muslim literature, including *The Rubaiyat*, by Persian poet Omar Khayyam and the stories of Ali Baba and Aladdin and the lamp as depicted in *The Arabian Nights*.

Extension

Interested students can read books about the Crusades or learn about the kings and sultans who were involved in these wars. For example, Saladin was a great ruler of the Saracens, and many interesting stories are available that describe his character. Many stories have also been written about King Richard the Lionhearted.

The Crusades

People who follow the teachings of the prophet Muhammad are called *Muslims*. In the eleventh century, the Muslims did not want Christian pilgrims to travel through their land to visit holy places.

This angered Pope Urban II, the head of the Christian church. The pope called for a Holy War against the Muslims to drive them out of the Holy Land. Five wars were fought between the Christians and the Muslims over the next 200 years. These wars were known as Crusades, or Holy Wars, because they were wars between two religions.

Many knights were eager to fight for the Holy Land. Some fought for God. Others enlisted because they wanted to bring back riches from the Holy Land.

Two leaders who fought each other during the Crusades were Richard the Lionhearted, King of England, and Saladin, the leader of the Saracens. The Saracens were the Muslim people who ruled most of the Holy Land.

During the Crusades, thousands of people died, both Muslim and Christian. The Christians won Jerusalem in the first war, but lost it again in the Second Crusade and never won it back.

In spite of the terrible losses, some good came out of these wars – the Christians and the Muslims met, and they learned from each other and traded goods. Long after the wars were over, people from the two regions were doing business together and sharing ideas.

Date:_____   Name: _____

The Crusades

Use these words to fill in the blanks in the sentences.

Holy Wars	Christians
Saladin	Jerusalem
Richard the Lionhearted	pilgrimages
Muslims	pope

1. Many people in medieval times made _____
   to the Holy Land.

2. The Holy Land included the city of _____.

3. The _____ called for a Holy War against the Muslims,
   because the Muslims were preventing Christians from making
   pilgrimages to the Holy Land.

4. The Crusades were also known as the _____ _____
   because they were wars between two religious groups in the
   Holy Land.

5. The Crusades were Holy Wars between the _____
   and the _____.

6. The leader of the Muslims was _____ .

7. The King of England during part of the Crusades was _____
   _____.

Trade Goods From
the Holy Land

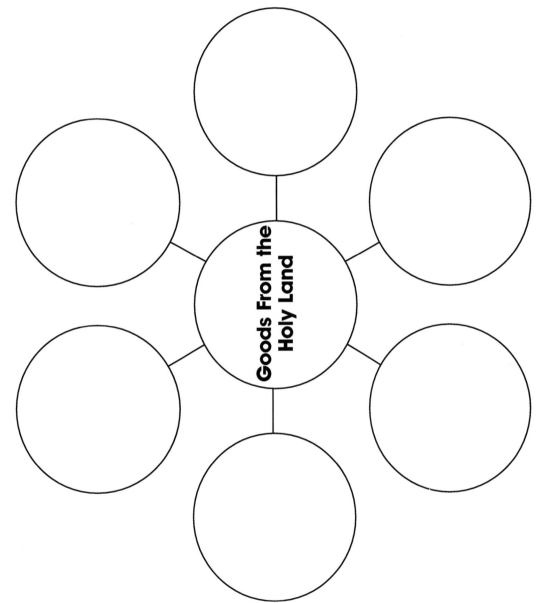

Goods From the
Holy Land

17 | The Magna Carta

Background Information for Teachers

During medieval times, countries were ruled by a monarchy. Monarchy means there is one ruler, a king or queen. The king's word was law; to disobey him was treason. When King John I of England was ruler, many people believed he abused his power by over-taxing his subjects, and fighting and losing too many wars. He also tried to take land away from the Church since he could not collect taxes from church land. In 1215, he was forced to sign the Magna Carta (Latin for "great charter").

The Magna Carta comprised 63 pages of demands by English barons (great lords) and bishops. Their demands were the beginnings of the development of democracy. From this point on, a monarch's powers were limited. Councils were formed that consisted of barons, bishops, and elected representatives from the knights and townspeople. These council meetings were called *parliaments* and were the beginnings of the government we have today. Women and serfs were excluded from council meetings and had little or no rights at all.

Materials

- information sheet titled, "The Magna Carta" (included. Make a copy for each student.) (1.17.1)
- time lines from lesson 2

Activity

Begin by comparing the role of kings in medieval times to how our country is run today. Ask:

- Who were the leaders of countries in medieval Europe? (kings)
- How did a king become leader?

- Who is the leader of our country?
- How did that person become the leader? (elected)

Explain that, originally, the first kings were successful warriors who won the right to be king by winning wars. Later, kings inherited the position from their fathers or mothers. Ask:

- Do we choose our leaders the same way?
- What do you think might happen if people in medieval times did not like their king?

Hand out the information sheet (1.17.1), and read it together. After reading the sheet, discuss the importance of the Magna Carta.

Have students mark the date of the Magna Carta on their time line from lesson 2. They can then complete the activity sheet.

Activity Sheet

Directions to students:

Read the information sheet again, then answer the questions on the activity sheet (1.17.1).

Extension

Research how the signing of the Magna Carta played a role in the beginnings of parliament. Near the end of the Middle Ages, council meetings were held to discuss the concerns of the people. Great Lords and bishops attended these council meetings, along with representatives of knights and townspeople. The parliament we have today in Canada got its start from these council meetings in medieval England.

Date:_____   Name: _____

The Magna Carta

In the 1200s, England was ruled by King John I. He was not a popular king. He made many mistakes in the way he ruled his country. King John fought – and lost – many wars with France. He attacked the Church and tried to take some of its land. This made the bishops and abbots very angry. He raised taxes over and over again until all the great lords and townspeople were also very angry with him. The great lords, or barons, and the bishops joined together against King John.

King John needed the support of the lords and bishops. In 1215, he agreed to the list of rights they had prepared. King John signed this agreement at a place called Runnymede, a meadow beside the Thames River, outside of London. This agreement is called *Magna Carta*, which means the "great charter." This charter forced the king to respect the rights of the different groups of people.

Some of the rights King John promised to respect were:

- the rights for the Church to choose its own bishops and keep its land
- the rights of the nobles to not have higher taxes unless a council voted for a special tax
- the rights of towns and cities
- the rights of free men to be tried by jury before they can be jailed or fined

By signing the Magna Carta, King John agreed that the king could no longer do whatever he wanted. From this time forward, people in England had some say in the way their country was ruled.

Date: _____

Name: _____

Magna Carta

Answer the questions in complete sentences:

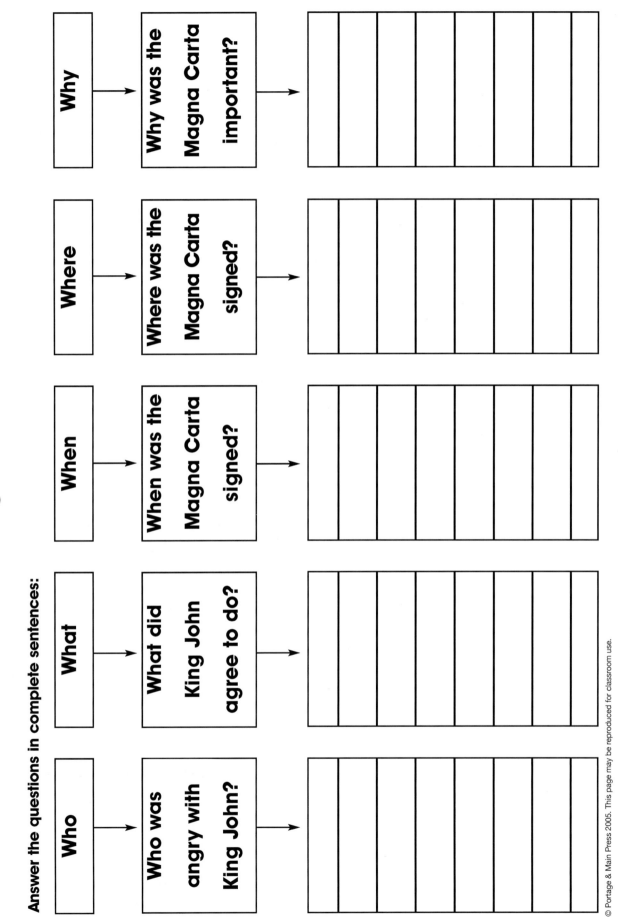

Who	What	When	Where	Why
Who was angry with King John?	What did King John agree to do?	When was the Magna Carta signed?	Where was the Magna Carta signed?	Why was the Magna Carta important?

18 | Culminating Activity: Medieval Festival

Note: To consolidate the information presented to students in this unit, students will research, organize, and prepare a medieval festival.

Background Information for Teachers

Fairs and festivals were an important part of life in medieval times. People lived hard lives, and they needed frequent opportunities to take a break from work and engage in games, feasts, and revelry.

The word *holiday* comes from the term *holy day*. There were many holy days in the Church calendar. Guilds and parishes also celebrated on a special day for their particular saint. Some medieval holidays were:

March/April	Easter
April 1	All Fool's Day
April 23	St. George's Day
May 1	Mayday
June 21	Midsummer's Eve
July 15	St. Swithin's Day
August 1	Lammas Day
September 29	Michaelmas
October 31	All Hallows Eve
November 1	All Souls' Day
	St. Catherine's Day
December 25	Christmas
	St. Stephen's Day
January 6	Twelfth Night
February 14	St. Valentine's Day

On holidays, peasants and serfs did not have to work. Instead, they went to special church services and afterwards participated in sports and dancing, and drank plenty of ale. Often, a grand feast was held at the lord's manor or castle. Everyone went. The important people sat at the high table, which was, literally, set higher than the rest.

Materials

- chart paper
- markers
- books that describe medieval fairs, feasts, and festivals (An excellent reference is *A Medieval Feast* by Aliki.)
- drawing paper
- pencils
- wooden dowels, 30 cm in length (one for each student)
- fabric scraps (including satin, brocade, wool, linen, burlap)
- wool
- Crayola Model Magic
- pipe cleaners
- Plasticine or Styrofoam
- paint
- paintbrushes
- glue guns
- markers
- information sheet titled, "A Medieval Feast" (included. Make an overhead transparency of this sheet.) (1.18.3)
- overhead projector
- "Medieval Feast Recipes" for gingerbread and custard tarts (included) (1.18.4)
- materials for medieval festival activities (will vary as selected by the class)
- food supplies and equipment (will vary based on recipes chosen by the class)

Activity: Part One: People at a Medieval Festival

Begin by reading excerpts from books about festivals, fairs, and feasts in medieval times. Discuss the types of games, performances, and other things that were done at these events, and record the students' ideas on chart paper.

Explain to students that they are going to plan and put on a medieval festival. Decide on a date (you may want to try to tie it to an ▶

actual holiday that would have been a festival day on the medieval calendar).

On chart paper, record students' suggestions as to who should attend the festival. Ask:

- Who would come to a medieval festival? (There would be the king, queen, lord, lady, steward, bailiff, serfs, lord mayor, craftsmen and craftswomen, apprentices, parish priest, knights, other noble friends of the lord and lady, and so on.) Make sure there are as many roles as there are students.

Explain to the students that each of them will be playing a role of one of the guests attending the feast. From the list, have each student select the person he or she wants to be. Record each student's name beside his or her role on the list.

Note: For characters such as the king, queen, and parish priest – only one student should select these (or you may wish to draw names). Other characters, such as knights and serfs, can be selected by several students.

The students will now have an opportunity to make a puppet character of the person they will be at the feast. Explain to the students that since they will be making actual three-dimensional models of the characters, it will be important to know what type of clothing they wore, as well as other information such as where they lived and their type of work. Distribute activity sheet A (1.18.1), along with a variety of books about medieval times. Have the students use the references to complete the sheet.

Activity Sheet A

Directions to students:

Write down the character you are making for the festival. As you gather information about your character, write it in point form on this page. When you are done, write some fictional information about your character on the bottom half of the page (1.18.1).

Note: Some students may decide to work together to portray a family group.

Activity: Part Two: Making a Medieval Character

Have the students follow these steps to create their medieval characters:

1. Draw: Have the students draw sketches of their medieval character before starting the figure. They should draw from pictures, and then create or change one of those drawings in some way to make their character look the way they want him or her to look (e.g., fat or thin, tall or short).

2. Make the frame: Use pipe cleaners as the frame for the figures. Make a "stick man" form out of pipe cleaners. A circle of pipe cleaner can be the head. Twist each piece of pipe cleaner together carefully so no bits of wires stick out.

3. Make the base: Place the dowel firmly into a chunk of Plasticine or Styrofoam, which will be the base. Now wire the pipe cleaner figure securely to the dowel in at least three places. The figure should be able to stand on its own. The pipe cleaner figure can now be posed into position as students choose.

4. Flesh out the figure: Begin to cover the pipe cleaner figure with Model Magic. This creates the flesh of the figure. Model Magic sticks to itself very well when wet, so more pieces can be added to build up certain areas like the nose and chin and stomach. Be sure all pipe cleaners are covered with Model Magic.

5. Add colour: Model Magic can be painted with watercolour, or even water-based markers. Have the students add colour to

18

all areas of their figures that will not be covered by clothing. This includes the flesh and facial features.

6. Clothe the character: After researching and sketching the clothes, have the students choose some suitable fabric scraps. Use a glue gun to attach the fabric to the figure to form clothes. These do not have to be exact. It is more important that students choose more colourful, richer fabric samples for nobility clothing, and rougher, duller wool fabric for peasants' clothing.

Note: Glue gun use should be carefully supervised by adults.

7. Add extra touches: Have the students add hair, hats, beards, and so on, using the materials provided.

Activity: Part Three: Writing in the First Person

After the students have completed their characters, have them use activity sheet B (1.18.2) to introduce their character to the rest of the class. This activity is an effective way for students to become well acquainted with their own and other medieval characters. Have them share these introductions with the class and discuss the characteristics and roles of each person in medieval society.

Activity Sheet B

Directions to students:

Write a paragraph that introduces your medieval character. Also draw a picture of the character (1.18.2).

Activity: Part Four: Festival Activities

The research that students have done to learn about their characters will help them to plan the activities for the festival. As a class, record a list of activities that took place at a medieval festival. For example:

- The nobles played chess and cards.
- Peasants played soccer and also enjoyed a game similar to Blind Man's Buff.
- People told jokes and sang and danced.
- They watched puppet shows and mystery plays.
- Some peasants wore masks and performed skits for food and money from the nobles. They were called *mummers*.
- Jugglers, gymnasts, and musicians entertained the people.

Plan several activities for the students to take part in during the class festival. Collect materials required for these activities, and have students participate in activities that their specific characters would do. Medieval-style music could also be played during the festivities.

The Feast

Selecting Food: As a class, discuss the types of food that were eaten in medieval times, and select some for your feast. Display the overhead of the medieval feast menu (1.18.3), and discuss the foods listed. Ask:

- Do we eat these foods today? Which ones?
- Which ones might we include in our feast?

Have students look on the Internet for medieval recipes. There are some that include rose petals cooked into the food. Recipes for gingerbread (the way it was made in the Middle Ages) and custard tarts are included with this lesson (1.18.4). Ginger ale is a good substitute for the ale people drank in medieval times.

Note: Be aware of food allergies when planning the class feast.

18

Arranging the Feast: Arrange desks or tables so that members of the nobility are at the head, or high, table. If possible their table should actually be higher that the rest. Students should help to organize the seating arrangement from the king and queen down to the lowly serf or beggar. Medieval models should be placed at each person's spot to remind everyone who he or she is.

Setting the Tables: In medieval times, large slices of stale French bread called *trenchers* were used as plates for the feast. Have students cut paper plates to look like a slice of bread. There were no forks for most of the Middle Ages – food was eaten with the fingers.

Serving the Food: Serfs and peasants served food, first to the nobility, then on down to the serfs and beggars.

Extension

Students may want to develop their medieval characters more fully by writing an adventure story set in medieval times that stars their character.

Assessment Suggestions

■ Observe students as they research and create their medieval characters. Look specifically at their ability to gather information and use this information in creating their figures. Use the anecdotal record sheet on page 13 to record results.

■ Have students complete the student self-assessment sheet on page 19 to reflect on their own learning about a medieval festival.

■ Evaluate each student's medieval glossary. Assess on the basis of number of entries and clarity of definitions.

Date:_____   Name: _____

My Character

1. In point form, record important information about your character.

My character is:_____

Information I have gathered about this type of person: _____

_____

Occupation: _____

Home: _____

Clothing: _____

Interesting facts:_____

_____

2. Record fictional details about your character.

Name: _____

Age: _____

Family: _____

Job: _____

Things I like to do: _____

_____

Problems I have had: _____

_____

_____

Other interesting facts about me: _____

_____

_____

Date:_____   **Name:** _____

Introducing...Medieval Me!

Write a paragraph to introduce yourself to the class.

Hello, my name is _____

_____

_____

_____

_____

_____

_____

A Medieval Feast

An actual menu from the fourteenth century

Boar's head with
brawn pudding

•

Shellfish scented with
jasmine, rosemary &
marigold

•

Fruit tarts

•

Salmon with orange

•

Sugared nuts

Stuffed quarter of bear

•

Sugared mackerel

•

Squirrel stew

•

Apple and figs

•

Cakes with honey

•

Wine with water or
Hot mulled wine

Medieval Feast Recipes

Gingerbread (very easy)

- 125 mL clear honey
- 1 loaf bread (450 g), at least 4 days old, grated and ground into fine crumbs (If bread is too fresh, it will not make sufficiently fine crumbs.)
- 5-10 mL each of ginger and cinnamon
- 1 mL ground white pepper (optional)
- pinch saffron, if desired

1. Bring the honey to a boil and skim off any scum.

2. Keep the pan over very low heat, and stir in breadcrumbs and spices.

3. When the mixture is a thick, well-blended mass, press firmly into a small, greased layer pan 20 cm square.

4. Cover and leave in a cool place several hours or overnight before turning out on a cake plate.

5. Cut into small slices to serve.

Honey and bread were common foods in most places. Spices such as pepper, ginger, and cinnamon were brought back to Europe by the Crusaders. From that time on, Europeans were always anxious to find a shorter or safer route to the East, where these spices were available. In a later period, Europeans would spend much time, money, and many lives to find a "Northwest Passage." In the course of their searches they "found" the New World, its people, and foods such as hot peppers, potatoes, tomatoes, and new kinds of corn.

Custard Tarts

Pies or tarts could have fruit filling or meat filling. This is the time when we get our rhyme "Four-and-twenty blackbirds baked in a pie." For special feasts, medieval cooks would use pastry to make castles and other structures.

- pastry for an open pie shell or 24 (or more) small tart shells
- 750 mL light cream or a combination of cream and milk
- 4 eggs (or 8 yolks, if you prefer)
- 125 mL sugar
- 1 mL salt

Optional:

- Pinch of saffron (for colour) or
- 1 mL almond extract or pinch each of cloves, ginger, mace or nutmeg, cinnamon (for flavour) or
- 125 mL to 250 mL chopped dates or other dried fruit or fresh strawberries

1. Beat eggs and sugar together.

2. Beat in cream and seasonings.

3. Pour into prepared pie shell or tart shells, over fruit (if fruit is used).

4. For one large tart, bake 10 minutes at 218°C; then about 30 minutes at 135-150°C.

5. For small tarts, bake about 20 minutes at 190°C.

This recipe often makes more filling than you expect, so it is a good idea to have extra shells available.

From: *People Through the Ages: Teachers' Guide* [Winnipeg: Peguis Publishers, 1992]

19 | Review Activities

Materials

- chart paper
- markers
- "Medieval Jeopardy Sample" (included) (for teacher use) (1.19.2)
- "Who Am I?" sample (included) (for teacher use) (1.19.4)

Note: Concepts can be reviewed at any time during the unit, using a variety of activities. Some examples are included in this lesson.

Activity One: Word Cycle

On chart paper, copy the word cycle sample (below). Distribute activity sheet A to the students. Instruct students to organize the words in the ovals so each is related to the words beside it in some way. Students can write in point form in the spaces between the ovals to explain how the words are related.

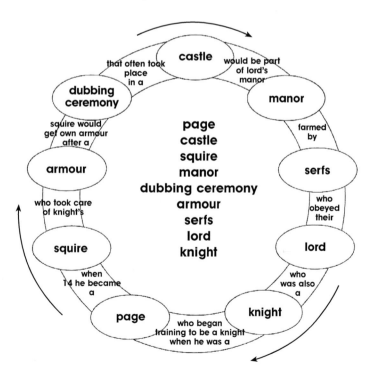

Activity Sheet A

Directions to students:

Organize the words in the ovals so each word is related to the words beside it in some way. Write in point form in the spaces between the ovals to explain how the words are related (1.19.1).

Activity Two: Medieval Jeopardy

Compose "answers" from the contents of this unit. (See 1.19.2 for sample questions and answers.) Students must give the "question" for the answer. After playing this a few times, have students create the "answers." This activity is a good, fun way for students to review new vocabulary and important concepts.

Activity Sheet B

Directions to students:

Create answers and questions using information you have learned in this unit. With a partner, take turns asking and answering the questions (1.19.3).

Activity Three: Who Am I?

Have students make up description cards for people in medieval society and read them to the class. Classmates must guess who he or she is. (See 1.19.4 for sample cards.)

Activity Sheet C

Directions to students:

Make up description cards for people living in medieval times. Read the cards aloud, and have classmates guess "Who Am I?"(1.19.5).

Word Cycle

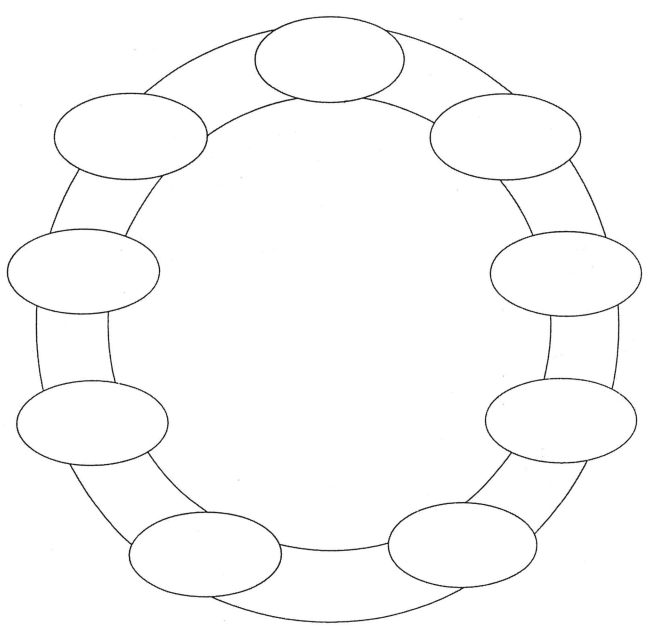

page	manor	serfs
castle	dubbing ceremony	lord
squire	armour	knight

Medieval Jeopardy
Sample Cards

Answer: This is a terrible epidemic that swept through medieval Europe.

Question: What is the bubonic plague or Black Death?

Answer: These are a series of wars between the Christians and Muslims in the Holy Land.

Question: What are the Crusades?

Answer: This is an important agreement signed by King John that gave people more rights.

Question: What is the Magna Carta?

Answer: This is the name of the religion that follows the teachings of the prophet Muhammad.

Question: What is Islam?

Answer: This is the trench filled with water around a castle.

Question: What is a moat?

Answer: This is a piece of land given by the king to a knight.

Question: What is a manor?

Answer: This is a medieval celebration with food and fun activities for everyone.

Question: What is a medieval festival?

Answer: This is a decorated book made by monks and nuns.

Question: What is an illuminated manuscript?

Medieval Jeopardy

Answer: **Question:**	**Answer:** **Question:**
Answer: **Question:**	**Answer:** **Question:**
Answer: **Question:**	**Answer:** **Question:**
Answer: **Question:**	**Answer:** **Question:**

Who Am I?

Clue:
I was dubbed by the king in a special ceremony.

(knight)

Clue:
By right, all land belongs to me. The great lords are my vassals.

(king)

Clue:
The serfs farm my land for me. I perform wedding ceremonies and funerals.

(priest)

Clue:
I serve at the lord's table. I had to leave my own home when I was seven. I am learning how to fight.

(page)

Clue:
I took vows and entered a convent. I can read and write, and I help people who are sick.

(nun)

Clue:
I work hard to farm the lord's land and my own as well.

(serf)

Clue:
I travel on a long journey with many others to the Holy Land.

(pilgrim)

Clue:
I serve a knight, polish his armour, and learn how to fight from him.

(squire)

Who Am I?

Clue:	Clue:
( )	( )
Clue:	**Clue:**
( )	( )
Clue:	**Clue:**
( )	( )
Clue:	**Clue:**
( )	( )

References for Teachers

Bagley, J.J. *Life in Medieval England*. New York: G. P. Putnam's Sons, 1960.

Buehr, Walter. *Knights and Castles and Feudal Life*. New York: G.P. Putnam's Sons, 1957.

Caselli, Giovanni. *History of Everyday Things, The Middle Ages*. New York: Peter Bedrick Books, 1988.

Day, Malcom. *The World of Castles and Forts*. New York: Peter Bedrick Books, 1995.

Furneaux, Jordan, R. *A Concise History of Western Architecture*. London, UK: Thames and Hudson, 1979.

Gibbons, Gail. *Knights in Shining Armor*. New York: Little, Brown and Co., 1995.

Gravett, Christopher. *Castle*. New York: Alfred A. Knopf, 1994.

———. *The World of the Medieval Knight*. New York: Peter Bedrick Books, 1996.

James, Alan. *Castles and Mansions*. Minneapolis: Lerner Publications, 1989.

Langley, Andrew. *Medieval Life*. New York: Alfred A. Knopf, 1996.

Lasker, Joe. *A Tournament of Knights*. Mexico: HarperCollins, 1986.

Macaulay, David. *Castle*. Boston: Houghton Mifflin, 1977.

Oakes, Catherine. *Exploring the Past: The Middle Ages*. London, UK: Hamlyn Publishing, 1989.

Oakeshott, Ewart. *A Knight & His Weapons*. London, UK: Lutterworth Press, 1971.

Smith, Beth. *Castles*. New York: Franklin Watts, 1988.

Sobol, Donald J. *The First Book of Medieval Man*. New York: Franklin Watts, 1959.

Spellman, Linda. *Castles, Codes, and Calligraphy*. Santa Barbara: The Learning Works, 1984.

Suskind, Richard. *Men in Armor, The Story of Knights and Knighthood*. New York: Grosset & Dunlap, 1968.

Taylor, Barbara. *World of Castles*. Owing Mills, MD: Ottenheimer Publishing, 2000.

Temple, Frances. *The Ramsay Scallop*. New York: HarperCollins, 1994.

Treece, Henry. *Know About the Crusades*. London and Glasgow: Blackie, 1963.

Unstead, R. J. *Looking at History, Book 2: The Middle Ages*. London, UK: A. & C. Black, 1969.

Canada and World Connections

Unit 2: Canada's Provinces, Territories, and Regions

Books for Children

Brown, Margaret Wise. *The Important Book*. New York: HarperCollins, 1977.

Gertridge, Allison. *Meet the Canadian Authors and Illustrators: 50 Creators of Children's Books*. Richmond Hill, ON: Scholastic Canada, 1994.

Harrison, Ted. *O Canada*. Toronto: Kids Can Press, 1992.

Kleitsch, Christel, and Paul Stephens. *Dancing Feathers* (rev. ed.). Toronto: Annick Press, 1988.

Kusugak, Michael. *Baseball Bats for Christmas*. Toronto: Annick Press, 1990.

Lee, Dennis. *Alligator Pie*. Boston: Houghton Mifflin, 1974.

MacKay, Kathryn. *Ontario*. Discover Canada series. Toronto: Grolier, 1991.

Montgomery, Lucy Maud. *Anne of Green Gables*. Toronto: Ryerson Press, 1955.

Sauer, Julia L. *Fog Magic*. New York: Viking Press, 1971.

Taylor, Barbara. *Maps and Mapping*. New York: Kingfisher Books, 1993.

Trottier, Maxine. *One Is Canada*. Toronto: HarperCollins, 1999.

Web Sites

- **www.canada.gc.ca/**

  Government of Canada's home page: click on "About Canada" for maps, facts and history, Canadian symbols, and more. With links to provincial and territorial primary web sites.

- **www.gov.on.ca/**

  Province of Ontario's home page: click on "About Ontario" for information and links to Ontario's history, cities and towns, population and culture, and natural resources. This site also includes maps of the different regions of Ontario.

- **www.tctrail.ca/**

  The Trans Canada Trail Site: includes the "Trail Story" (what it is, its route, benefits of the trail), a "Progress Report," photo stories, libraries, and much more.

- **www.cln.org/**

  Community Learning Network: click on "Theme Pages" and scroll down to Famous Canadians. ("Theme Pages" are organized alphabetically. Click on the letter *F* for "famous" to begin your search.) An excellent resource for teachers.

- **www.ec.gc.ca/envhome.html**

  Environment Canada's Green Lane home page: click on "Regional Sites" and then "Ontario" for programs on topics such as The Great Lakes, Community Resources, Events, and Weather Watching.

- **www.weatheroffice.com/**

  Environment Canada's Weather Office: click on "Sky Watchers," a program on weather for elementary school teachers and students. Includes an Ontario home page.

- **www.oagee.org/**

  Ontario Association for Geographic and Environmental Education: provides hundreds of links to related organizations such as *Canadian Geographic* and The Federation of Ontario Naturalists. This site also provides links to maps, Ontario's parks, and regional news.

- **www.flora.org/globaled/**

  Global Education Network is an online directory of resources for use in the curriculum. Click on "Environment" (listed under "Categories") for links to Canadian Global Change Program, Canadian Wildlife Federation, David Suzuki Foundation, Rideau Valley Conservation, and many other environmental organizations.

Introduction

In this unit, students will develop their understanding of Canada's provinces and territories. They will identify and locate the physical regions within the provinces and territories, and investigate the economies of these regions. They will also learn about the structure and functions of provincial government.

Integrated exposure to the concepts introduced in this unit will help to solidify students' understanding of the provinces and territories. Many of the activities rely on a large collection of pictures of Canadian landscapes. Some excellent sources of pictures and information are:

- calendars
- postcards
- magazines
- tourist brochures, pamphlets, and videos

A collection of road maps, community maps, wall maps, and atlases will also be of value during this unit.

Consider establishing a Canadian Corner in your classroom. Provide research material such as books and magazines, along with Canadian artifacts such as national and provincial flags and symbols, examples of minerals and rocks from the various regions, as well as Canadian coins and stamps.

Social Studies Vocabulary

Throughout this unit, teachers should use, and encourage students to use, vocabulary such as: *region, Canadian Shield, Appalachians, Great Lakes Lowlands, St. Lawrence Lowlands, Hudson Bay Lowlands, interior plains, Arctic Lowlands, Cordilleras, physical features, boundaries, province, capital, territories, natural resources,* and *grid*.

Materials Required for Unit

Classroom: index cards, markers, pencils, calculator, tape, chart paper, coloured pencils, 30-cm rulers, Post-it Notes (small), globes (several), tag board, construction paper (large sheets), glue, scissors, Bristol board, metre stick, blue mural paper, ledger-sized paper, lined paper, nonpermanent overhead pens, clipboards, transparency sheets, highlighters, black construction paper, photocopy paper, paintbrushes

Books, Pictures, and Illustrations: *Meet Canadian Authors and Illustrators: 50 Creators of Children's Books* (a book by Allison Gertridge), map of Canada, wall map of Ontario, library books, newspapers, graph paper (included), map of Canada showing longitude and latitude (included), landscape pictures of Canada (from calendars and magazines), physical map of Canada, atlases (1 per student), resource material about Canadian provinces, territories, and regions, *The Important Book* (a book by Margaret Wise Brown), map of Canada showing population density, reference material on the St. Lawrence Seaway, municipal maps with grid system, tourist information on Ontario (brochures, pamphlets, posters), Ontario road maps, resources material about environmental issues

Equipment: Internet access, TV, pedometer, overhead projector, access to photocopier

Other: large basket, tokens (5 per student), 4 cups or bowls, food items (e.g., loaf of bread, can of apple juice, can of vegetables), materials for creating map collages (e.g., gravel, leaves, tinfoil, grass, twigs), materials for making landscape models (e.g., clay, cake pans, soil, sand, small stones, jar lids), water, sponges, toothpicks, 2 colours of bingo chips (1 per student), paper bag, baseball caps or canvas painter hats, fabric paints, shoeboxes

1 Ongoing Activities

Note: To develop a true Canadian connection, consider correlating this unit with other subject areas. Introduce the activities that follow at the beginning of this unit. Work on one or more of the activities daily to build on the concepts being introduced throughout the unit.

Materials

- *Meet Canadian Authors and Illustrators: 50 Creators of Children's Books*, a book by Allison Gertridge
- index cards
- markers
- large basket
- pencils
- map of Canada
- wall map of Ontario
- pedometer
- calculator
- library books
- Internet access
- TV
- newspapers
- graph paper (2.1.3)

Activity One: Canadian Authors and Illustrators

Use the book, *Meet Canadian Authors and Illustrators*, by Allison Gertridge, to make biography cards on Canadian authors and illustrators. Display one biography card each day. Have students locate the person's place of birth and current hometown on a map of Canada. These can be marked with a number and connected to a legend. Use the birthdate to calculate the person's age. Challenge students to locate the author's or illustrator's books in the library.

Activity Sheet

Directions to students:

Identify and describe the Canadian setting that is in the book you are reading. Use a new activity sheet for each setting you describe (2.1.1).

Activity Two: Canadian Settings

Start a Canadian book basket. As students read books, have them identify and discuss any Canadian settings that are in the book. Use the activity sheet to record information (2.1.1).

Activity Three: Trans Canada Trail

On a wall map of Canada, mark the trail across the country. As a class, calculate the total distance of this trail.

For a field trip excursion, walk a portion of the trail nearest your community. Also consider fundraising activities to support the completion of the trial. Check out the Trail Web Site <www.tctrail.ca>.

Activity Four: Read Across Canada

On a map of Canada, mark the approximate location of the Trans Canada Trail. Record the number of pages that students read in books written by Canadian authors. Count each page as one kilometre. Use the data to mark a trail across the country. Set reading goals based on arriving at specific locations on the trail.

Activity Five: How's the Weather?

Select one Canadian community from each province and territory. With information from web sites, television weather channels, or the newspaper, record daily temperatures in each community. Divide the class into working groups, and have each group graph the temperature in one of the communities (see 2.1.2). Discuss and compare the temperatures in these regions.

▶

1

Activity Six: Favourite Canadians

Have students mark the home towns or present community of their favourite Canadian singers, dancers, musicians, and athletes. They can also research these Canadians and write up biocards that can then be displayed around the map with connections made with a piece of yarn.

Canadian Settings

Colour the setting location on the map:

Title: _____

Author: _____

Canadian Location: _____
_____

Description of the Canadian Setting:

_____

_____

_____

_____

Read by: _____

- ✂ - - - -

Colour the setting location on the map:

Title: _____

Author: _____

Canadian Location: _____
_____

Description of the Canadian Setting:

_____

_____

_____

_____

Read by: _____

Date:_____ **Group #:** _____

2 | Introduction to Canada

Background Information for Teachers

In this lesson, you will introduce students to the concepts of country, region, population, resource, economy, government, and taxes. Use the following definitions:

Country: an area of land that has its own government and definite boundaries

Region: an area of land that has some common characteristics (in geography, regions have similar geographic aspects, e.g., prairie grasslands, boreal forest)

Population: the number of people living in an area

Resource: a material that can be used and sold

Economy: the ways that a group makes and spends money

Government: a system by which people rule themselves and their land

Taxes: what a population contributes to the government to pay for the things that everyone shares and needs

In this lesson, students also begin to review mapping concepts, including the purpose for maps and key parts of maps (title, legend, compass rose, pictorial symbols).

Materials

- 5 tokens per student (e.g., paper tickets, bingo chips, Popsicle sticks)
- tape (to divide the room into quadrants)
- chart paper and markers (for recording observations)
- cups or bowls (one per quadrant)
- 4 cards (each listing one of the four cardinal directions: north, south, east, west)
- masking tape
- wall map showing a compass rose and boundary lines (provincial, territorial, or country)
- coloured pencils
- 30-cm rulers

Note: Before you begin the lesson, divide the room into quadrants using tape as floor markings. Each quadrant should include some student work areas and some classroom resources (door, carpet area, pencil sharpener, supplies, and so on). It is not necessary or preferable to have an equal number of students or resources in each quadrant.

Activity: Part One: Token Games

Record the terms *government, country, region, population, taxes, resources*, and *economy* on chart paper. Have the students read the words and discuss their current understanding of each term.

Note: This is only an introduction to the terms. The definitions will come later in the lesson.

Ask students to note the new divisions in the room. Tell them that these areas are the new regions of the classroom. Ask:

- How many students are in your region of the classroom?

Explain that the number of students in the region is that region's population. Tell students that you will give each group a number of tokens. This amount will be five times the number of students in that region. Ask students to calculate the number of tokens they should receive. When the groups have given you this calculation, place each group's total number of tokens in a container located somewhere in each of the four regions. On chart paper, record the number of tokens that each group starts with.

Explain to the students that every time a student from another region enters their region to use something (a "resource" such as the pencil sharpener, door, computer, or books), that student must place a token in their container.

▶

Continue with other classroom activities for a block of time (story time, work time, recess). As the game continues, certain issues will arise as students move among the regions. Discuss these ideas as they come up. For example:

- the group that owns the door will get rich at recess and gym time
- a group with few "resources" will run out of money
- groups with larger populations will start off richer
- resources such as the pencil sharpener and large-group area become money makers
- students will make decisions to live without some items. Some become necessities, others luxuries.

Once the students have played the token game for a period of time, stop the game. Have the groups total the tokens that they now have in their possession. Record these totals on the chart paper. Have students discuss the process of the game. Ask:

- Was this game fair?
- What items were used in each region?
- How did groups gain tokens? Lose tokens?
- Should the door be owned by one group?
- If the door is owned by everyone, who will pay for repairs?
- How could you share the cost of these repairs?
- Who will make decisions about the door? Everyone? Representatives? One person?
- How could you solve the problem of one group running out of tokens?

During this discussion, certain understandings will begin to surface. Record these ideas on chart paper. For example:

- each area of the classroom had its own characteristics (regions)

- each region had a specific number of people (population)
- each region had items that other groups needed (resources)
- the need for resources caused people to gain and lose tokens (economy)
- certain items needed to be accessed by everyone all the time
- these items could be owned by the whole class (country)
- representatives could make decisions for these items (government)
- group-owned items would need to be maintained with everyone's tokens (taxes)

Discuss how this game is somewhat like the way our country is run. Refer back to the chart of terms and discuss how these terms relate to the game, as noted above.

Note: This is a very introductory-type discussion. Some concepts will come more quickly than others. Other concepts will be referred to throughout the unit.

Distribute activity sheet A (2.2.1) to the students. Encourage students to work with a few other students from their region to complete the first page of the activity sheet. Then, on the second page, have them continue to work together to complete the third column of the chart, connecting the definitions to the token game and recording their ideas. When students finish this task, have them share their answers. As a class, discuss real-world connections that students may come up with, and have them record these in the last column of the chart.

Refer back to the list of terms on the chart paper, and record definitions for these terms. Display these terms and definitions for reference throughout the unit.

▶

2

Activity Sheet A

Note: This is a two-page activity sheet.

Directions to students:

On the first page, record the tokens that each group started and ended with, draw a diagram of your region, then answer the questions. On the second page, read each word and its definition. Discuss how this word relates to the token game. Record your ideas in the third column (2.2.1).

Classroom Discussion: How do you think these ideas are used in the real world? Record your ideas in the last column of the chart (2.2.1).

Activity: Part Two: Mapping

Hand out copies of activity sheet B (2.2.2). Review the parts of the map presented on the sheet: title, compass rose, and legend. Explain to students that they will be making a map of the token game. Brainstorm appropriate titles for the map. Have students title the map. Locate the cardinal directions in the classroom, and display the cards identifying each direction by taping them to the four classroom walls.

Have students design a compass rose for this map. Have them refer to the compass rose on the wall map.

Have the students begin by drawing the classroom boundaries in coloured pencil. They should then add a short coloured line to the legend to represent the classroom boundaries. Next, have the students identify and shade in the four classroom regions using four different coloured pencils. These colours should also be added to the legend.

Discuss the idea that maps are usually drawn from a bird's-eye view, and that symbols are used to indicate items on a map. As an example, work together to decide how a certain item, such as the door, will be represented on

the map. List this item in the legend, along with the symbol decided upon. Give students plenty of time to complete the map.

Activity Sheet B

Directions to students:

Draw a map of the token game. Make a title and a compass rose. Draw boundaries for the classroom, then identify and colour in the four regions. Draw symbols to show resources in each region. Complete the legend to show the classroom boundaries, as well as all regions and resources (2.2.2).

Activity Centre

Have students search through newspapers to find articles that include the words they studied. Make a bulletin board display with the articles. Highlight the words in the articles.

Assessment Suggestions

- Observe groups as they discuss the definitions during Activity: Part One. Focus specifically on students' ability to work together to complete the task. Use the cooperative skills teacher assessment sheet on page 18 to record results.

- As a class, identify criteria for the token game map. These may include:
  - accurate compass rose
  - accurate boundaries for classroom and regions
  - accurate placement of symbols on the map
  - complete legend

Record these criteria on the rubric on page 16, and record results while reviewing the students' maps.

Date: _____   **Name:** _____

Token Game

Tokens	Group 1	Group 2	Group 3	Group 4
Starting Amount				
Ending Amount				

Draw a diagram of your region of the classroom:

What was the population of your region? _____

What were your main resources? _____

_____

An advantage of our region was _____

_____

A disadvantage of our region was _____

_____

Word	Definition	Token Game	Real World
country	an area of land that has its own government and definite boundaries		
region	an area of land that has some common characteristics		
population	the number of people living in a given area		
resource	a material that can be used and sold		
economy	the ways that a group makes and spends money		
government	a system by which people rule themselves and their lands		
taxes	what a population contributes to the government to pay for the things everyone shares and needs		

Date: _____

Name: _____

Title: _____

Legend		
Symbol	**Item**	
	classroom boundaries	
☐	region	
☐	region	
☐	region	
☐	region	

3 Starting With What We Know

Materials

- large map of Canada
- small Post-it Notes
- definitions on chart paper (from lesson 2)

Activity

Begin by discussing the token game from the previous lesson and the terms introduced in that lesson. Refer to the chart for the definition of a country. Use the map of Canada as a focal point for discussion. Display the map. Ask:

- What country do you live in?
- What colours do you see on this map?
- What do they represent?
- What types of lines do you see on this map?
- What do they represent?
- During the token lesson we divided our classroom into regions. What are the parts called that Canada is divided into?
- What province do we live in?
- What are the names of the provinces in Canada?
- What are the names of the territories in Canada?
- Which provinces or territories are larger than ours? Which are smaller than ours?
- Which provinces or territories have been visited by students in the class?

Mark the provinces or territories that students have visited with Post-it Notes, and identify the students who have been there. These students could become a primary source of information when researching the provinces.

Divide the class into working groups, and provide all students with the activity sheet (2.3.1). Have the students work together to complete the first two columns of the KWL chart.

Note: The third column of the chart can be completed by students during the unit, as they gain new understandings.

Activity Sheet

Directions to students:

In the first column of your chart, record some things that you already know about Canada. In the second column, list some things that you would like to know about Canada. During this unit, complete the third column of the chart with things that you learn about Canada (2.3.1).

Extensions

- On chart paper, list questions that students have recorded in the second column of their KWL charts. Sort the questions into *skinny* questions and *fat* questions: skinny questions require only a yes or no answer; fat questions involve a more complex answer. Challenge students to rewrite *skinny* questions to make them *fatter*.

- Research the symbols on Canadian coins. Contact Canadian Heritage for more information.

Activity Centre

Encourage students to bring in Canadian artifacts for Canadian Corner. Items may include reference books, atlases, maps, T-shirts, souvenirs, postcards, and pictures from family trips. Post a daily question from the students' KWL charts in the Canadian Corner. Challenge students to research answers, and display them at the centre.

Date: _____

Name: _____

A Canadian KWL

What I Know About Canada	What I Want to Know About Canada	What I Have Learned About Canada

4 Canada's Land Regions

Background Information for Teachers

Canada is divided into regions based on the physical characteristics of the land. Different sources often name the regions differently, or break the regions into sub-regions. For the purpose of introducing students to the regions, use the following: Appalachians, Hudson Bay Lowlands, Arctic Lowlands, Great Lakes/St. Lawrence Lowlands, Interior Plains, Cordillera, and Canadian Shield.

Note: Some physical maps of Canada may name the regions differently; for example, the Arctic Lowlands are sometimes referred to as the North region. If the maps and/or atlases in your classroom list terms different from those used here, discuss this issue with students. It provides them with a valuable lesson in geographical terminology.

The student information sheets in this lesson give an overview of each region, and the map identifies the location of each region. The definitions are fairly simplistic; students will be able to focus on the differences between the regions. You may want to encourage some students to research the regions in more depth as an extension activity.

Materials

- various landscape pictures of Canada (calendars or magazines are a great source for these. Be sure to include pictures from different regions of the country.)
- blank vocabulary cards (cut from tag board)
- large sheets of construction paper
- glue
- Post-it Notes
- physical map of Canada (wall map or atlases)
- information sheets titled, "Canada's Land Regions" (included. Make a copy for each student.) (2.4.1)
- chart paper
- map titled, "Canada's Land Regions" (included) (for teacher reference) (2.4.3)

- markers
- coloured pencils

Activity: Part One: The Canadian Landscape

Note: Prior to the actual lesson, establish a bulletin board or area in the room where landscape pictures can be displayed.

Display a variety of landscape pictures for the students to examine. Challenge them to find various ways to sort the pictures. Sorting rules may include:

- seasons
- water/land
- main colours
- vegetation
- physical land characteristics

Divide the class into pairs or triads. Have each group choose a landscape picture, then provide the groups with several blank vocabulary cards. Have students work in groups to brainstorm words that are inspired by the picture; for example, *cold, lonely, trees, flat, forest, wild.* Encourage students to include both descriptive words and feeling words. Have the groups record each word on a vocabulary card.

Now select one of the landscapes yourself. With the students, brainstorm words that describe the picture, and record these words on vocabulary cards. Use the cards to model for the students how they can arrange words to make poetry. For example:

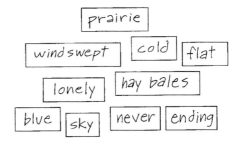

▶

Have the groups choose some of their own words to create a poem about their landscape picture. When students are happy with their poem, have them glue the words onto construction paper. Call on each group to present its poem and picture. Display the pictures and poems on the bulletin board.

Activity: Part Two: Reading Nonfiction

Refer to the landscape pictures displayed on the bulletin board. Discuss the fact that although the pictures are all Canadian landscapes, each has very different physical characteristics. Explain that the huge size of Canada means that it includes many different types of landforms. Each landform has specific characteristics. Explain to students that they will be reading a description of each land region in Canada and making notes on the important characteristics of each region.

Review note-taking strategies. Remind students to record only key words and phrases, not to copy whole sections.

Divide the class into pairs of students. Provide each pair with "Canada's Land Regions" information sheet (2.4.1) and activity sheet A (2.4.2). Have the groups follow the reading and note-taking instructions and complete the activity sheet. Provide sufficient working time.

Once the groups have completed this research, have groups share and discuss their findings. Record the information on chart paper and post in the classroom.

Now refer back to the landscape pictures on the bulletin boards. Provide each student with two Post-it Notes. Have each student choose two pictures and, using the information from their information sheet and activity sheet, predict which land region the pictures are from. Instruct students to write the land region on the Post-it Note and place on the picture. (Not every picture needs a Post-it Note; some pictures will be easier to identify than others. The number of Post-it Notes will illustrate this.)

Activity Sheet A

Note: This is a two-page activity sheet.

Directions to students:

Decide who will be partner A and who will be partner B. Partner A will read those sections on the information sheets (2.4.1) marked Reader A. While Partner A is reading, Partner B is the listener. Partner A reads the first section aloud, then turns over the paper. Partner B tells Partner A what he or she heard about the land region. Now Partner A and B work together to record important words or information in the note-taking section for that land region. Partner B reads the next section. Partner A tells Partner B what he or she heard and then they work together to make notes. Repeat this process until the activity sheet is completed (2.4.2).

Activity: Part Three: Identifying Land Regions on a Map

Display the physical map of Canada. Refer to the parts of a map discussed in previous lessons (e.g., compass rose, title, boundaries, legend). Discuss the legend on the physical map of Canada. Ask:

- What do the colours mean?
- What parts of the country do the different regions cover? (Use directional words.)
- Which region is the largest?
- Which region is the smallest?
- Which region is the most northern?
- Which region are we in?

4

Now focus on the climate in the different region. Ask:

- Which region is in Canada's far north?
- What is the climate like in this region?
- Why is it colder up north?
- How is the climate different in each region?

Use the facts on the information sheet (2.4.1) to discuss and compare the climate in the various regions. Have students underline or highlight the appropiate sentences in each paragraph.

Provide students with activity sheet B (2.4.4). Assign each student one of the seven regions. Have each student identify that region on the map, then colour in the region on the activity sheet. Indicate what the colour means in the legend. Using the notes from activity sheet A, have students record, in sentences, what they know about their region. When students have completed their sheets, arrange the class into groups of seven, with one student from each land region in each group. Have the students in each group share their maps and research.

Activity Sheet B

Directions to students:

Record your land region at the top of the page. Using information from the wall map or atlas, identify and colour in your region. Record the colour and the region in the legend. Using your notes from activity sheet A, write some complete sentences about your land region. Include its location in Canada, the landforms you would find in it, waterways, climate, and any other information you have (2.4.4).

Extension

Have students sketch a landscape on blank paper with pencil. Provide other media such as glue and chalk, pastels, watercolours, and pencil crayons to create landscape drawings. Introduce drawing concepts such as perspective and horizon line.

Note: *Perspective* is a point of view – drawing accurately from a particular vantage point to give the appearance of three-dimensions. The *horizon line* is the edge where the sky meets the ground.

Activity Centre

Place landscape pictures and blank vocabulary cards in a box. Encourage students to use the pictures to create more poetry for the bulletin-board display.

Assessment Suggestion

Observe students as they work in pairs to take notes on Canada's land regions. Focus specifically on their ability to listen for pertinent information and record ideas. Use the anecdotal record sheet on page 13 to record results.

Canada's Land Regions

Reader A:

Appalachians

The Appalachian region is found on the east coast of Canada. It includes some parts of Nova Scotia, Prince Edward Island, New Brunswick, Newfoundland, and Quebec. The land is characterized by low mountains and plains. The climate is cool and wet, with a hurricane tendency in the summer and early fall. The area was once covered with lakes, which left behind good soil for farming. Farms in this area produce potatoes, milk, apples, and maple sugar. The forests are mixed – aspen, maple, ash, spruce, pine, and hemlock all grow in the region. The forests are used for pulp and paper production and lumber. Coal and oil are found in the region. The Appalachians are home to some of Canada's best fishing.

Reader B:

Hudson Bay Lowlands

The Hudson Bay Lowlands is a small strip of land that encircles the southwest coast of Hudson Bay and the west coast of James Bay. This land is flat and marshy. Large boulders and rocks punctuate the swamps. The area has long, cold winters and short, warm summers.

Reader A:

Arctic Lowlands

This region is located north of the Arctic Circle and the tree line. Short, cool summers and long, cold winters help to maintain permafrost on the land. The southern part of this area has small hills; the northern part has mountains, glaciers, plains, and islands. Very little vegetation grows in this area. Oil, gas, lead, zinc, and silver can be found in this region.

Reader B:

Interior Plains

Parts of Manitoba, Saskatchewan, Alberta, British Columbia, Yukon, and the Northwest Territories are in the Interior Plains. The region has short, hot summers and long, cold winters. The land has large grassy prairies, kept almost treeless by violent prairie fires. Farmers now use this land to produce grain and to raise livestock. It is the largest farming area in the world. Many fossil deposits, along with oil, natural gas, coal, potash, quartz, clay, and sulphur, have been found underground in the Interior Plains.

Reader A:
Cordillera

This mountain region is found on the west coast of Canada, west of the Interior Plains. The Cordillera covers six mountain ranges, including the Rocky Mountains. This region also has high plateaus, meadows, fjords, valleys, and glacial ice fields. The coastal area is flat. The highest parts of this region have little precipitation while the lower parts are snowy, cool, and rainy. The oldest coniferous trees in Canada are found in this region. The two main forests are the Western coastal forest and the boreal forest. The main industries are forestry, fishing, hydroelectricity, and orchards and vineyards.

Reader B:
The Great Lakes/St. Lawrence Lowlands

This lowlands region is in southeastern Ontario and Quebec bordering the Great Lakes and Newfoundland. This area was shaped by glaciers. The land has plains and hills including the Niagara Escarpment, which is a steep rise of rock separating two levels of flat land. This region has the longest growing season in Canada. The summers are hot and humid with many thunderstorms. The winters are cool and snowy. The forests are mixed and include walnut, oak, sugar maple, and hemlock. The majority of Canada's manufacturing takes place in this region. It also includes the St. Lawrence Seaway.

Reader A:
The Canadian Shield

The Canadian Shield is an area of ancient rock. This huge rock structure is the remains of mountains that were eroded by retreating glaciers. These glaciers also left thousands of hollows that have become lakes. The rock is covered by a thin layer of soil; fir and spruce trees grow here. The northern areas of the Canadian Shield have long, cold winters and short, warm summers. The weather is cool and wet. Many of the towns in this region were originally populated by people who were mining or working in forestry or hydroelectricity plants.

Canada's Land Regions: Note–Taking

Appalachians

Hudson Bay Lowlands

Arctic Lowlands

Interior Plains

Cordillera

The Great Lakes/St. Lawrence Lowlands

The Canadian Shield

Canada's Land Regions

Legend

▦	Appalachians	▨	Great Lakes/ St. Lawrence Lowlands
▨	Arctic Lowlands	■	Hudson Bay Lowlands
⣿	Canadian Shield	▨	Interior Plains
▨	Cordillera		

0   500   1000 km

Date: _____   Name: _____

Canada's Land Regions

Land Region: _____

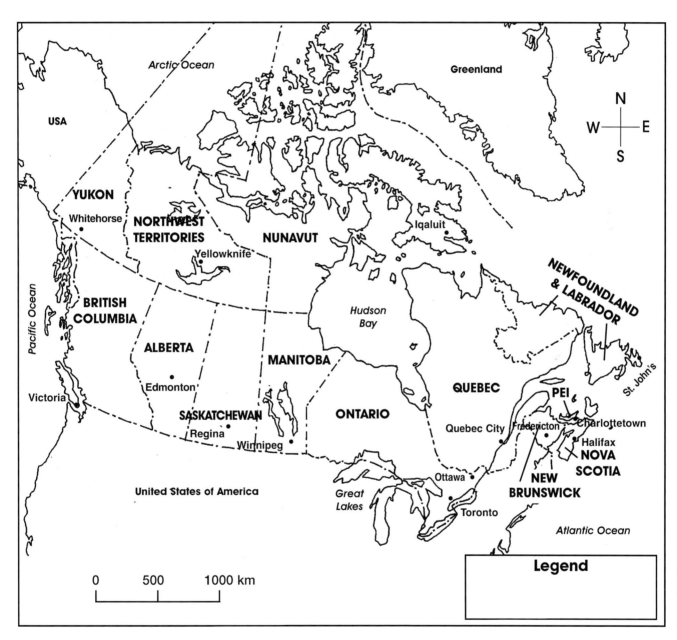

_____

_____

_____

_____

5 | Overview of the Provinces and Territories

Background Information for Teachers

The information sheet, "Canada's Provinces and Territories" (2.5.1), presents an overview of the provinces and territories. You will find basic information you can use with the whole class. More in-depth information can be obtained from other sources located in your Canadian Corner, at bookmarked web sites, and on CDs.

For quick reference: Canada has ten provinces and three territories. Each province and territory has its own government, with similar powers. There is one main difference between provinces and territories: provinces maintain responsibility for their natural resources; the federal government is responsible for territorial natural resources. The leader of both provincial and territorial governments is called a *premier* (except in Quebec).

Provinces/Territories and Their Capitals:

British Columbia	Victoria
Alberta	Edmonton
Saskatchewan	Regina
Manitoba	Winnipeg
Ontario	Toronto
Quebec	Quebec City
Newfoundland & Labrador	St. John's
New Brunswick	Fredericton
Nova Scotia	Halifax
Prince Edward Island	Charlottetown
Nunavut	Iqaluit
Northwest Territories	Yellowknife
Yukon	Whitehorse

Materials

- large wall map of Canada
- coloured pencils
- information sheet titled, "Canada's Provinces and Territories" (included. Make a copy for each student.) (2.5.1)
- labels of provinces and territories (included. Make a copy for each group.) (2.5.4)
- scissors
- glue
- drawing paper
- black construction paper
- pencils

Activity: Part One: Canada's Provinces and Territories

To help students develop an understanding of the relationship between a country and its provinces and territories, begin the lesson by discussing the school community. Ask:

- What is the name of your school?
- Who is in charge of the whole school?
- Where do decisions about the whole school take place?
- What rules are followed by the whole school?
- What parts of the school are used by everyone?
- What are the smaller regions of the school called?
- Who is in charge of this classroom?
- Do we have other rules to follow that are specific to this classroom?
- Do you think other classrooms have different rules?

Explain that in some ways a school is similar to a country. A school is a large physical space with a person in charge (the principal). The school is divided by boundaries (walls) into classrooms. The classrooms are similar to the provinces and territories. They are smaller regions with another person in charge (the teacher).

Distribute activity sheet A (map of Canada) (2.5.2), along with coloured pencils and graphite pencils. Explain to students that decisions made for the whole country are

▶

5

made in the capital city of Ottawa. Identify Ottawa on the large wall map. Have students locate Ottawa on their maps. As a class, decide on a symbol that will represent the capital of the country. This symbol could be a star or a specifically coloured circle. Have students mark the symbol on their map, then include it in the legend.

On the large wall map trace the boundaries of Canada with your finger or a pointer. Have the students trace this boundary on their maps with a specific colour. Now have them note the symbol in the legend by drawing a short coloured line.

Explain that the other parts of the map belong to another country, the United States of America. Identify the international boundary between Canada and the U.S.A., and have students draw this boundary on their maps with a different colour. Have students note the symbol in the legend.

Now trace the provincial and territorial divisions. Have the students trace a line that will represent the provincial and territorial boundaries, using a different colour. Have them include the symbol in the legend.

Explain that these boundaries are different from the boundaries of the physical regions of Canada. The regions' boundaries are physical divisions, based on the features of the land. The provinces' and territories' boundaries were decided upon as a way of dividing up the country.

Cover or remove the wall map of Canada. Explain to the students that you will be providing them with an information sheet about the ten provinces and three territories of Canada (2.5.1). Challenge them to use the written information to label the provinces,

territories, and capital cities. Although some students may already know some of this information, encourage them to use the written material to check their facts. Remind them that they are using these sources to locate specific information. Encourage them to skim read for those specifics. Give students the choice of working alone or with a partner, as this activity addresses different learning styles. Provide sufficient time to work.

When students have completed this task, display the wall map of Canada to check work.

Activity Sheet A

Directions to students:

You have been given a map of Canada. Together, we have used lines to show the country's boundaries, as well as international, provincial, and territorial boundaries. We have also marked Canada's capital city, Ottawa.

Read the information sheets on the provinces and territories (2.5.1). Try to find the information that tells you where each province and territory is located in Canada, and what each capital city is. Use this information to label the province or territory and its capital city. You may already know some of the information. If this is the case, use the information sheets to check your answers. You may work alone or with a partner (2.5.2).

Activity: Part Two: The Canadian Cycle

Explain to the students that during this next activity, they will reinforce their learning about Canada's provinces and territories, and will look for ways that the provinces and territories are alike. They will create a word cycle using the information sheet from Activity: Part One (2.5.1).

▶

5

Divide the class into working groups. Provide each group with the information sheet (2.5.1), activity sheet B (2.5.3), the provinces and territories labels (2.5.4), as well as scissors and glue. Have the groups cut out the labels.

Have the groups place the word *Ontario* in one of the circles on the cycle. Ask:

- Can you think of a way that Ontario is similar to another province? (Accept any answer that has a factual rationale. For example, both Ontario and Quebec are in eastern Canada.)

Place the label for that province in the next circle. Now, connect that province to another. Suggest that students not glue any labels until the cycle is complete. There are many connection possibilities, and changes may have to be made to make a complete cycle. Have students arrange all the provinces and territories around the cycle in a way that they can connect each one to another. For example:

> Manitoba—prairie province—Saskatchewan—capital city named after a queen—British Columbia—coastal province—Nova Scotia...

When students feel that they have completed the cycle, have them glue the labels in place and use the connecting bars to explain the connection. Have groups share the cycles with the class, then display the cycles in the classroom.

Activity Sheet B

Note: Copy this sheet onto large ledger-sized paper to provide more room for labels.

Directions to students:

Cut out the labels of the provinces and territories (2.5.4). Place the labels on the circles of the word cycle so that each label relates to the one next to it on the cycle. Write words on the bars of the cycle to explain how the labels are related (2.5.3).

Activity: Part Three

Select three provinces/territories with significantly different climates (e.g., Ontario, British Columbia, and Nunavut). Use weather web sites or newspaper articles to track daily weather in the three regions.

▶

5

Activity: Part Four

Using drawing paper and pencils, have students practice drawing outline maps of various provinces or territories. Assign students different provinces/territories, and have then draw an outline on black construction paper and cut it out. Display the maps and challenge the class to identify each province/territory by shape.

Extensions

■ Provide copies of provincial flags or shields. Have students place the flags on the cycle sheet, connecting common elements (e.g., lion, maple leaf, pattern, colour). Have students research the meaning of the symbols, and write the meaning on the connecting bars.

■ Math extension: Graph the population of each of the provinces and territories.

■ Create a time line that shows the date that each province and territory joined confederation.

■ Challenge students to identify the latitude and longitude boundaries of each province and territory.

Canada's Provinces and Territories

British Columbia

The most western province in Canada is British Columbia. It is the third largest province. British Columbia's coast is on the Pacific Ocean. Victoria, the capital city, is located on the south end of Vancouver Island. About 4 million people live in British Columbia. British Columbia has been a province since 1871.

Forests cover over half of this province, and forestry is the largest industry. British Columbia also has a large fishing industry. The province also produces apples, cherries, and plums. Copper, coal, gold, silver, and zinc are mined.

Alberta

Alberta is located between the Rocky Mountains and Saskatchewan. It is home to almost 3 million people. Alberta is considered one of the three Prairie provinces. It became a province in 1905. Alberta was once covered with ancient lakes; today, many fossils and dinosaur remains can be found where the lakes used to be. These remains have become fossil fuels (oil and natural gas).

Alberta is the main producer of oil in Canada. It is also the main producer of natural gas and coal. Potash, quartz, and salt deposits are found in Alberta. Other important industries are cattle farming, wheat farming, and forestry. The capital city is Edmonton.

Saskatchewan

Located between Manitoba and Alberta, Saskatchewan is the only Canadian province whose borders are not defined by a natural landform. About 1 million people live here. Regina is Saskatchewan's capital city. Saskatchewan became a province in 1905.

Saskatchewan is Canada's main producer of wheat. Other crops include barley, oats, canola, and flax. The province also produces oil, coal, and natural gas. It is a large producer of uranium and potash.

Manitoba

Manitoba became a province in 1870. It is home to 1 million people. Manitoba has a large French-speaking community. The capital city is Winnipeg. Manitoba is located in the centre of Canada, between Saskatchewan and Ontario. Even though Manitoba is an interior province, it has a coastline on Hudson Bay.

Manitoba is a producer of hydroelectricity. Wheat is Manitoba's main crop. Other crops include barley, oats, flax, and canola. Nickel, gold, copper, zinc, and gypsum are mined.

Ontario

Canada became a country in 1867. That same year, Ontario became a province. Canada's second largest province is home to 11 million people. Toronto is Ontario's largest city and its capital. Ontario is found north of the Great Lakes and west of Quebec.

Most of Ontario's population lives in an area called the Golden Horseshoe. This area is important because it has many industries (e.g., auto industry) and businesses (e.g., financial). The auto industry provides jobs for many Ontarians in this area. Many fruits and vegetables are produced here. Ontario also has a pulp and paper industry. Nickel, cobalt, salt, and magnesium are mined in northern Ontario. Ottawa, the capital city of Canada, is located in Ontario.

Quebec

Quebec, Canada's largest province, is home to more than 7 million people. Quebec is a French-speaking province. Its capital is Quebec City. Located east of Ontario, Quebec became a province in 1867.

Quebec has many natural resources. It has built huge hydroelectric plants and is a main producer of electricity. Pulp and paper and lumber are important industries. Gold, copper, silver, zinc, nickel, and asbestos are mined. Quebec farmers produce dairy products, livestock, fruits, and vegetables. Maple syrup is produced from large maple tree farms.

New Brunswick

New Brunswick is a producer of lead, zinc, and coal. Along with forestry, New Brunswick industries include fishing and farming. New Brunswick grows potatoes, apples, blueberries, strawberries, and cranberries.

New Brunswick is located east of Nova Scotia. Fredericton is the capital. New Brunswick's population is 740 000. New Brunswick became a province in 1867.

Nova Scotia

Nova Scotia, which became a province in 1867, is made up of mainland Nova Scotia and Cape Breton Island. It has a population of 900 000. The capital city is Halifax. The province is surrounded by the Atlantic Ocean, the Bay of Fundy, and the Northumberland Strait.

Fishing is an important industry. Nova Scotia also has a pulp and paper industry and fish packaging factories. Coal is mined and oil is produced. Farms grow Christmas trees and raise cattle for dairy products.

Prince Edward Island

Prince Edward Island is home to Canada's largest potato crop. It has a large fishing industry. The province also produces fertilizer, wood products, and medical supplies. Prince Edward Island's main industry, however, is tourism. People from all over the world come to visit Green Gables. All of this takes place in Canada's smallest province.

Prince Edward Island, or P.E.I., is located north of Nova Scotia and east of New Brunswick. It became a province in 1873. Its capital city is Charlottetown. The province has a population of 135 000.

Newfoundland & Labrador

Newfoundland became a province in 1949. It was the last province to join Canada. It is the most eastern province in Canada. It is made up of two parts, the island of Newfoundland and the mainland territory of Labrador. About 551 000 people live in Newfoundland. The capital city is St. John's. It is Newfoundland's largest city.

Oil is Newfoundland's main resource. It also produces and sells hydroelectricity and pulp and paper. Nickel, copper, zinc, lead, silver, limestone, and iron ore are all mined in Newfoundland.

Yukon

The Yukon Territory is the smallest of Canada's three territories. It is located north of British Columbia and west of the Northwest Territories. The total population of the Yukon is about 30 700. Most of the population lives in Whitehorse, the capital city. The Yukon became a territory in 1898.

The Yukon's main industry is mining. Its natural resources include gold, lead, zinc, and silver. The Beaufort Sea, which is directly north of the Yukon, is drilled for oil. Tourism, fishing, and fur trapping are other important industries in the Yukon.

Northwest Territories

The Northwest Territories became a territory in 1870. Since then, the Yukon and Nunavut territories have been created from land that once belonged to the Northwest Territories. The Northwest Territories is located between the Yukon and Nunavut. Yellowknife is the capital city. The population of the Northwest Territories is about 42 500.

The fur trade is an important industry in the Northwest Territories. There is little farming because of the permafrost. Diamonds, gold, zinc, lead, and silver are mined.

Nunavut

In 1999, Nunavut became Canada's newest territory. The most eastern territory, it borders Manitoba, Ontario, and Quebec to the south. Nunavut has a large amount of land, but only about 25 000 people.

Iqaluit is Nunavut's largest town and its capital. Nunavut's greatest resources are its land and its wildlife. Fishing – especially for whitefish and arctic char – is an important industry. Although Nunavut has deposits of copper, lead, silver, zinc, iron, gold, and diamonds, the permafrost makes mining difficult.

Canada

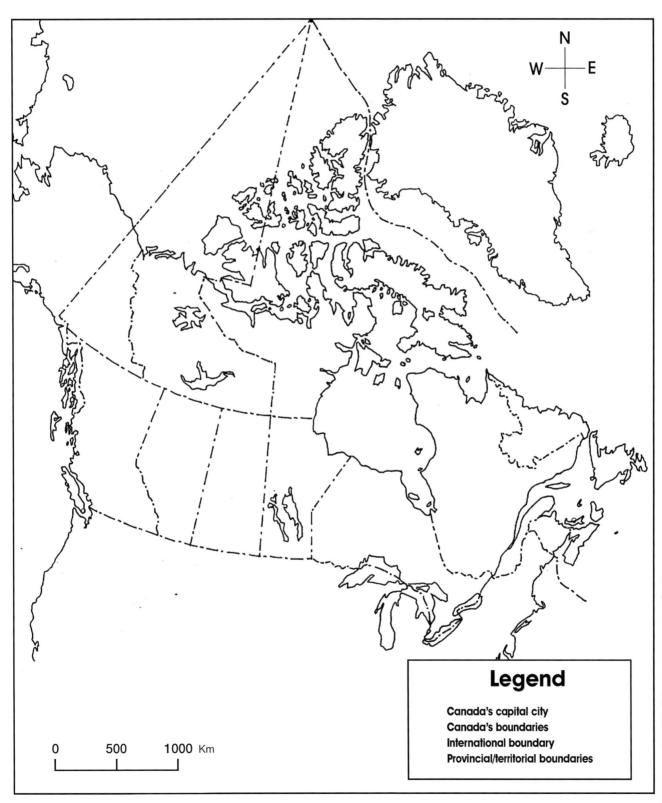

N
W — E
S

Legend

Canada's capital city
Canada's boundaries
International boundary
Provincial/territorial boundaries

0   500   1000 Km

Provinces and Territories Cycle

Labels: Provinces and Territories

Alberta	British Columbia	Manitoba
Ontario	Prince Edward Island	Nova Scotia
Newfoundland & Labrador	Nunavut	Quebec
Saskatchewan	Northwest Territories	Yukon
	New Brunswick	

6 Canadian Products

Materials

- chart paper
- markers
- variety of food items (e.g., loaf of bread, can of vegetables, apple juice. (Ensure that these food items have listed ingredients on their packaging. Collect one food item per working group.)
- chart titled, "Major Resources in Canada" (included. Make a copy for each student.) (2.6.1)

Note: The resource chart provides a quick reference for the main resources and industries in each province and territory.

Activity

Begin the lesson by reviewing the token game once again (see lesson 2). Refer to the resources that each quadrant had that other groups needed, and discuss how the groups exchanged resources/goods for tokens.

Explain that what happened in the token game is, in some ways, similar to how the economy of Canada works. Ask:

- What does the term *economy* mean? (the ways that a group makes and spends money)

Explain that the exchange of goods and services between provinces and territories creates the economy. The economy is the earning and spending of money. Record the term *economy* on chart paper and determine a class definition for this term.

Refer to the information sheet on the provinces and territories used in lesson 5. Explain that each province and territory has certain strengths for growing and/or producing materials. Those things that exist naturally in a region are called *natural resources*. Record this term on the chart paper and determine a class definition for this term. Ask:

- What are some natural resources that we have in Canada? (e.g., water, trees, nickel)

Brainstorm a list of natural resources to add to the chart.

Explain that things made or processed in a region are called *products*. Explain that products made or processed in a region are called *industry*. Record the term *industry* on the chart, along with a class definition. Ask:

- What are some industries that we have in Canada? (e.g., automobile manufacturing, food processing)

Stress that the sharing and exchanging of resources between the provinces and territories is important to Canada's economy. It allows us to have the things we need, and to produce things to sell around the world.

Now divide the class into working groups. Provide each group with a food item, along with activity sheets A and B (2.6.2, 2.6.3), and the "Major Resources in Canada" chart (2.6.1). Have students list the ingredients in their food item on activity sheet A (2.6.2). Point out that ingredients are listed based on the relative amount of each ingredient in the food item (first ingredients listed are the main ingredients). Also have students describe the packaging of the food item, including what the packaging is made from. Now have the groups use the "Major Resources in Canada" chart to locate as many of the ingredients and packaging materials as possible, and list the provinces/territories that could have participated in the making of the item.

Now have the groups title the map of Canada (activity sheet B, 2.6.3) with the name of the food item. Have them colour in the provinces and territories that they listed as participants in the production of the item.

Hands-On Social Studies • Grade 4

6

Finally, have the students reflect on this activity by completing the Learning Response on activity sheet A.

Activity Sheet A

Note: This is a two-page activity sheet.

Directions to students:

Use the activity sheet to identify the ingredients in your food item, the materials in the packaging, and the provinces/territories that may have participated in the production of this food item. After completing your map (2.6.3), reflect on what you have learned from this activity (2.6.2).

Activity Sheet B

Directions to students:

Title the map with the name of your food item. Colour in all provinces and territories that could have participated in the production of this food item (2.6.3).

Extensions

- As a class, identify all ingredients in the food items that were not listed on the chart. Use other resources (books, web sites, encyclopedias) to identify what these everyday ingredients are and where they may have been produced.

- Have students write an advertisement for an all-Canadian product. This could be a recipe that includes ingredients found in many provinces.

- Have students use Play-Doh, model magic, or small objects to build a model of a dinner table that has been served an all-Canadian meal. Have students write the menu for The Canadian Café.

Activity Centre

Place several other food items at the centre, along with the "Major Resources in Canada" chart and a large map of Canada. On Post-it Notes, have students record ingredients with a pictorial symbol and place the Post-it Notes on the map of Canada.

Assessment Suggestion

Review the students' activity sheets to see if they have accurately identified locations on the map where food ingredients may have come from. Use the anecdotal record sheet on page 13 to record results.

Major Resources in Canada

Alberta
- oil
- gas
- coal
- potash
- quartz
- salt
- cattle
- wheat
- forestry

British Columbia
- forestry
- apples
- cherries
- plums
- copper
- gold
- silver
- zinc
- fishing

Saskatchewan
- wheat
- uranium
- potash
- barley
- oats
- canola
- flax

Quebec
- aluminum processing
- maple syrup
- hydroelectricity
- pulp and paper
- forestry
- dairy products
- fruits and vegetables

Manitoba
- hydroelectricity
- nickel
- wheat
- barley
- gold
- oats
- flax
- copper
- canola
- zinc
- gypsum

Ontario
- pulp and paper
- plastics
- nickel
- cobalt
- auto industry
- salt
- fruits and vegetables
- magnesium

Newfoundland & Labrador
- oil
- hydroelectricity
- pulp and paper

New Brunswick
- potatoes
- apples
- blueberries
- strawberries
- cranberries

Nova Scotia
- fishing
- dairy products
- fish packaging
- coal
- oil
- Christmas trees

Prince Edward Island
- potatoes
- fish
- fertilizer
- wood products
- medical supplies

Yukon
- fur
- oil
- fish
- zinc
- gold
- lead
- silver

Nunavut
- fish processing
- copper
- lead
- silver
- zinc
- iron
- gold
- diamonds

Northwest Territories
- fur
- diamonds
- gold
- zinc
- lead
- silver

Date:_____   Name: _____
_____
_____
_____

What Are We Eating?
Where Does It Come From?

1. Our food item is _____

2. List the ingredients in the food item: _____

_____

_____

_____

_____

_____

_____

3. Describe the packaging that the food item comes in.

   What is the packaging made of? _____

_____

_____

_____

_____

_____

_____

_____

_____

4. Identify where in Canada the ingredients and packaging may have come from.

Ingredient	Possible Participants

5. On the map of Canada (2.6.3), colour all the provinces and territories that may have participated in the making of this food item.

6. Learning Response: What did you learn from this activity?

_____

_____

_____

_____

_____

_____

_____

_____

_____

_____

Date: _____   **Name:** _____
                                              _____
                                              _____
                                              _____

Food Item:_____

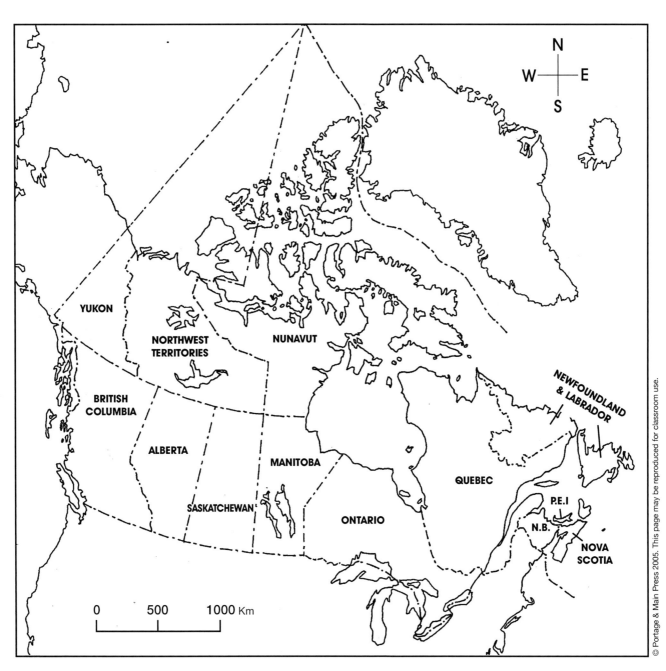

7 | Researching Canada's Provinces and Territories

Materials

- chart paper
- markers
- resource materials related to Canadian provinces, territories, and regions (e.g., nonfiction books, CDs, bookmarked web sites)
- blank paper for drawing maps
- Venn diagram (included. Make an overhead transparency of this sheet.) (2.7.4)
- overhead projector

Activity: Part One: Researching the Provinces and Territories

Explain to the students that they are going to research a Canadian province or territory. Ask:

- What do you think you should include in this research?

As a class, brainstorm a list of things that should be included in the research, and record these on chart paper. For example:

- a map of the province or territory
- its physical characteristics
- its economy (natural resources, industry)
- its population
- its climate
- its culture (e.g., recreation, special events)
- information sources used

Provide each student with activity sheets A and B (2.7.1, 2.7.2), blank paper to draw maps on, and a variety of reference materials on Canada's provinces and territories. Allow students plenty of time to gather information. Also allocate time for students to present their findings to their classmates.

Activity Sheet A

Directions to students:

Each day, use the Time-Management Record to record how much time you spent on your research, and describe what you did (2.7.1).

Activity Sheet B

Note: Copy several extras of this sheet. Students are to use one sheet for each source they use for information-gathering.

Directions to students:

Use the chart to record the source you used (books, CDs, web sites) and to record notes under each heading (2.7.2).

Activity Sheet C

Note: This is a four-page activity sheet.

Directions to students:

Cut out and staple the booklet then record and illustrate your province/territory research (2.7.3).

Activity: Part Two: Comparing the Provinces and Territories

Display the Venn diagram on the overhead (2.7.4). Explain to the students how they can use the diagram to compare and contrast things. As an example, use the Venn diagram to sort the students by who have brothers and who have sisters. Label the two boxes underneath the circles with the words *brothers* and *sisters*. List the names of all students who have only brothers in the first circle. Now list the names of the students who have only sisters in the second circle. Record the names of students who have both brothers and sisters in the intersecting set. The Venn diagram may also have a complementary set of those students who have neither brothers nor sisters. List these students on the outside of the diagram.

Explain to students that they will now use their research notes (2.7.2) from Activity: Part One to compare and contrast two provinces or territories. Pair up students who have studied different provinces/territories. Try to make as many different combinations of research as possible.

▶

7

Give students some time to discuss the research with each other. Provide activity sheet D. Have the students label the two connecting circles with the name of the province or territory that each researched. Have them use the diagram to record things that the two regions have in common in the intersecting area and things that are different in the main circles.

Note: Explain that the province/territory map will not have a complementary set. The students will only be putting on information that they found to be true for at least one of the provinces or territories.

When the students have completed their Venn diagrams (2.7.5), have them share their findings with the class, highlighting a few similarities and differences between the two provinces/ territories.

Activity Sheet D

Directions to students:

Share your research with a partner. Watch for similarities and differences between your provinces or territories. Record those similarities and differences on the Venn diagram (2.7.5).

Extensions

- The research notes from this lesson can be extended into a full research project by having students use their notes to write a report or to present their information as a visual display on a backboard.

- Conduct specific research on one of the territories to determine how technology has changed the lives of people in this region (e.g., snowmobiles, Internet access).

Assessment Suggestions

- As a class, develop criteria for the oral presentations of research. These may include:
  - clear speaking voice
  - accurate map of the province or territory
  - details on physical characteristics, economy, population, climate, and culture
  - identified sources

  List these criteria on the rubric on page 16, and record results during presentations.

- Have students complete the student self-assessment sheet on page 19 to reflect on their own learning while conducting the research project.

Date:_____   Name: _____

Time–Management Record

Keeping My Research on Track
Province or Territory:_____

Date	Length of Time	What I Accomplished

Date:_____   Name: _____

Topic:_____

Source: _____

_____

Heading	Research Notes
Physical Characteristics	
Economy	
Climate	
Culture	
Population	

Map of _____

-------------------------------------- ✂ ------------------

Facts About: _____
by: _____

Economy

Physical Characteristics

Culture

Climate

About the Researcher

_____

_____

_____

_____

_____

_____

Population

_____

_____

_____

_____

_____

Resources

_____

_____

_____

_____

_____

Other Interesting Facts and Illustrations

1.	2.
3.	4.

Name: _____

Date: _____

Venn Diagram

Comparing Two Provinces/Territories

8 | Ontario's Land Regions

Background Information for Teachers

Of the seven geographic regions in Canada, three exist in the province of Ontario: Canadian Shield, Great Lakes/St. Lawrence Lowlands, and Hudson Bay Lowlands. The largest land region is the Canadian Shield, sandwiched between the Great Lakes/St. Lawrence Lowlands to the south and the Hudson Bay Lowlands to the north. The student map (2.8.2) identifies the locations of these three landforms.

Materials

- information sheet titled, "Canada's Land Regions" and maps (see lesson 4)
- Ontario landscape pictures, divided into pictures that clearly represent the three regions (calendars or postcards are a good source for these)
- small, blank vocabulary cards
- Bristol board
- glue
- variety of materials for creating map collages (e.g., gravel, leaves, tinfoil, plastic wrap, grass, twigs)

Note: Students can participate in the collecting of these materials.

Activity: Part One: Ontario's Landscape

Review the land regions of Canada. Refer to the information sheet and the maps that the students created in lesson 4. Ask:

- Which land regions exist in Ontario?
- How would you describe the location of each?
- What do you remember about each region?

Divide the class into working groups. Provide each group with a set of pictures of one land region. You may have to have two or three groups working on the same region. Ask students to identify which land region their

pictures represent. Confirm that the students have chosen the correct region.

Have students use the blank vocabulary cards to record words that describe their pictures and region. Have the students sort the words. Sorting suggestions may include alphabetical order, nouns/adjectives, endings, and so on.

Have the groups of students display their landscape pictures, identify the land region, and share their vocabulary words with the class. Encourage other students to add descriptive words for each set of pictures.

Activity: Part Two: Creating Land Regions

Now that students are aware of the different types of landscapes in Ontario, provide them with copies of activity sheets A and B (2.8.1, 2.8.2). As a class, read each description of the land region from activity sheet A. On the map (activity sheet B), have students note where the land region is located.

Explain to the students that they are going to create a three-dimensional map of Ontario, using real materials to show its land regions. Have the students brainstorm materials that could represent each region. For example:

- tinfoil or plastic wrap to represent swampy water in the Hudson Bay Lowlands
- grass to represent the plains of the Great Lakes/St. Lawrence Lowlands
- gravel and stones to represent the Canadian Shield

Have the students decide on the material that they will use on their map for each region, and note it on activity sheet A (2.8.1). Encourage students to participate in the gathering of materials that they will need for this activity.

When materials have been collected, have the students glue the map onto a piece of Bristol

▶

Hands-On Social Studies • Grade 4

board to make it sturdy. They can then use their selected materials to cover the map in collage fashion. Ensure that the students include a legend on their maps.

Activity Sheet A

Directions to students:

Read the descriptions of each land region in Ontario. Select a material that you could use to represent this region on the map (2.8.1).

Activity Sheet B

Directions to students:

Glue your map onto Bristol board. Use your selected materials to cover each land region on the map. Include a legend on your map (2.8.2).

Extension

Use the vocabulary word cards from Activity: Part One to create poetry around the border of a map of Ontario.

Assessment Suggestion

Conference with students individually. Have the students explain the reason they chose each material. Use the individual student observations sheet on page 14 to record results.

Ontario's Land Regions

Hudson Bay Lowlands

A small strip of land encircles part of Hudson Bay and James Bay. This land is flat and marshy. Large boulders and part of rock punctuate the swamps. This area has long, cold winters and short, warm summers.

A good material to represent this region would be:

The Great Lakes/St. Lawrence Lowlands

This lowlands region is found in southeastern Ontario. It borders Lake Erie, Lake Ontario, and the St. Lawrence River. This area was formed by glaciers. The land has plains and hills, including the Niagara Escarpment, which is a long and steep rise of rock separating two levels of flat land. The region has the longest growing season in Canada. The summers are hot and humid with many thunderstorms. The winters are cool and snowy. The forests are mixed and include walnut, oak, sugar maple, and hemlock. The majority of Canada's manufacturing takes place in this region.

A good material to represent this region would be:

The Canadian Shield

The Canadian Shield is an area of ancient rock. This huge rock structure is the remains of mountains that were eroded and shaped by retreating glaciers. These glaciers also left thousands of hollows that have become lakes. Fir and spruce grow in the thin layer of soil that covers the rock. The northern area of the Canadian Shield has long, cold winters and short, warm summers. The weather is cool and wet. Many of the people living here work in hydroelectricity plants or in mining
and forestry.

A good material to represent this region would be:

Ontario's Land Regions

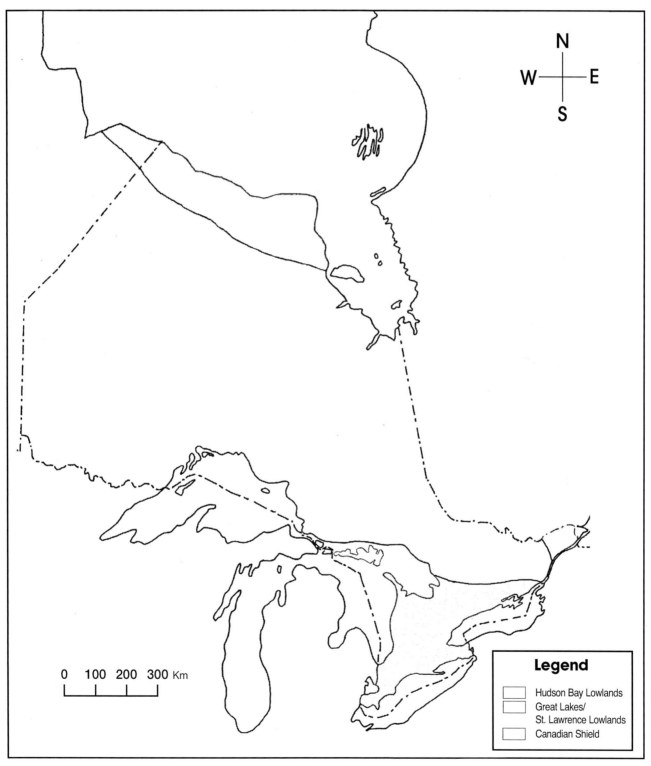

N
W — E
S

0   100   200   300 Km

Legend

Hudson Bay Lowlands
Great Lakes/
St. Lawrence Lowlands
Canadian Shield

9 The Great Lakes

Background Information for Teachers

The five Great Lakes are among the most important natural resources in the world. Lakes Superior, Michigan, Huron, Erie, and Ontario, together with the St. Lawrence River, form the world's largest freshwater ecosystem. The St. Lawrence River, which connects the Great Lakes to the Atlantic Ocean, can be seen from space. This area is home to over 40 million Canadians and Americans who use the water system for recreation, transportation, drinking, industry, power, and many other purposes.

The Great Lakes were formed by huge glaciers approximately 14 000 year ago. The five huge holes are filled with 18 quadrillion litres of melted water. The Great Lakes are in a state of constant change. They continue to be affected by nature through erosion, movement in the Earth's crust, and climate change. A more detrimental change is caused by the human use of the lakes. Toxic substances in the lakes have reached problematic levels, endangering the countless species of animals and plants that make their home in this huge ecosystem.

Materials

- chart paper
- markers
- information sheet titled, "Notes on the Great Lakes" (included. Make a copy for each student.) (2.9.1)
- supplementary research materials: books, bookmarked web sites
- atlases
- *The Important Book*, a book by Margaret Wise Brown
- wall map of Ontario
- metre stick
- road maps of Ontario
- Great Lakes grid sheets (included. Make a copy for each student.) (2.9.4 – 2.9.8)
- large sheets of graph paper
- scissors
- blue mural paper

Activity: Part One: Facts About the Great Lakes

Begin by creating a concept web on lakes. Print the word *Lakes* in the centre of a sheet of chart paper, and circle it. Brainstorm and organize words and phrases that describe what the students know about lakes. For example:

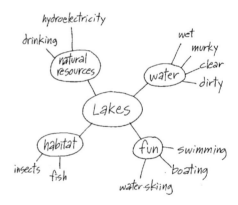

This web can be added to as students conduct research.

Now explain to the students that they are going to study a very important group of lakes called the *Great Lakes*. Provide students with the information sheet about the Great Lakes (2.9.1). Explain that the sheet provides some brief notes on each of the Great Lakes. The students' job is to create a paragraph about each lake based on these notes. Model this process for students. For example:

- The first note under Lake Huron says: "second largest Great Lake." How can we record that as a complete sentence?

Record on chart paper "Lake Huron is the second largest of the Great Lakes."

9

You may wish to continue with other examples until you are sure that students understand the task. Another option is to have students work in groups for each lake and record the sentences together on chart paper.

Assign sufficient working time for students to complete the paragraphs. If students finish early, have them refer to the reference books and web sites to confirm the facts in their paragraphs, and to include additional information they may find.

Have students share their work aloud. Refer back to the concept web on lakes. Add any information about lakes that the students have learned from this activity.

Activity: Part Two: Locating the Great Lakes

Distribute activity sheet A (map of Ontario) (2.9.2). Have students locate the Great Lakes. Then have them use their paragraphs and information sheet (2.9.1) to predict which lake is which. Use the atlases to confirm predictions and label the lakes. Challenge students to locate and label other bodies of water in Ontario, such as Hudson Bay, James Bay, Georgian Bay, and the St. Lawrence River. Ask:

- Have you ever looked up at a cloud and thought its shape reminded you of something else?
- If you saw a cloud in the shape of Lake Ontario, what else would the shape remind you of?

Continue the game for the other four lakes. Record suggestions on chart paper. This activity will help visual learners remember the names of the lakes.

Activity Sheet A

Directions to students:

Locate and label each of the five Great Lakes on the map. Also label other bodies of water on the map (2.9.2).

Activity: Part Three: The Importance of the Great Lakes

Read *The Important Book* (by Margaret Wise Brown). With the students, identify the pattern of the book. Together write another page that could go in the book. For example:

> The important thing about recess is that we get to go outside. It is fun, it gives you time to play with your friends. You can use the time to go to the washroom. But the important thing about recess is that we get to go outside.

When students are comfortable with the pattern, tell them that they are going to write an important paragraph about one of the Great Lakes. Assign students one of the lakes. Hand out activity sheet B (2.9.3). Review the pattern of the activity sheet. Have students refer back to their paragraphs and information sheet from Activity: Part One. Provide sufficient time for students to complete the assignment, and give students an opportunity to share their work.

Activity Sheet B

Directions to students:

Select one of the Great Lakes. On the activity sheet, write some of the important things about this lake (2.9.3).

▶

9

Activity: Part Four: Map Scales

Display the wall map of Ontario. Ask:

- How big is Ontario on this map? (use a metre stick to check estimates)
- Is this how big Ontario really is?

Discuss with students that maps are drawn to scale. This means that everything on a map is shrunk, or scaled down, by the same amount. Scales make sure that things that are bigger than something else in real life are bigger on a map as well. Provide students with some examples of scales on road maps or atlases. Refer back to the Great Lakes on the Ontario map. Ask:

- Which lake is the largest? (Lake Superior)
- Which lake is the smallest? (Lake Ontario)
- Which lakes are most similar in size? (Lake Michigan and Lake Huron)

Distribute the Great Lakes grid sheets (2.9.4 – 2.9.8). Explain to students that they are going to make larger models of the lakes by enlarging them to scale. This way they will still be able to tell which is largest and which is smallest. Model this for one of the lakes. Discuss the scale of the lake on the graph paper, counting the squares in different directions. Then, as a class, determine how the lake would be drawn to scale on a large sheet of graph paper.

Divide the class into pairs of students. Provide each pair with a large sheet of graph paper, pencils, and markers. Have the students select one of the lakes to draw to scale, ensuring that at least one pair of students is drawing each of the five lakes. Ask the students to identify which lake they are drawing and title the graph paper. Stress to students that each small square on the grid sheet is equal to one large square on the graph paper. Allow sufficient time to complete the activity.

Once students have completed the large outlines of the Great Lakes, have them cut out the lakes and trace the outline of their lake onto blue mural paper.

Have the students mount their activity sheet (2.9.3) onto an appropriate lake outline. Display the work in the Canadian Corner.

Extensions

- Have students do more in-depth research on the Great Lakes. Create a trivia board game about the Great Lakes.

- Research the projects that are underway to clean up the Great Lakes. Challenge students to get involved by writing letters or creating posters that promote the clean up.

Assessment Suggestion

Observe students as they draw the scale drawings of the Great Lakes. Watch specifically for accurate measurements. Use the anecdotal record sheet on page 13 to record results.

Notes on the Great Lakes

Lake Huron
- second largest Great Lake
- has 30 000 islands
- surrounded by world's largest limestone quarries
- receives water flow from Lake Superior and Lake Michigan
- known as "lake in the middle"
- water stays for 22 years (retention time)

Lake Erie
- shallowest and warmest Great Lake
- 95 percent ice-cover in the winter
- suffers greatest stress from industry, people, agriculture
- retention time is 3 years

Lake Superior
- world's largest freshwater lake
- largest, deepest, and coldest Great Lake
- large enough and deep enough to hold all of the other Great Lakes
- least polluted
- retention time is 200 years

Lake Michigan
- third largest Great Lake
- only Great Lake that is entirely in the United States
- retention time is 100 years

Lake Ontario
- smaller and deeper than Lake Erie
- many industrial centres located on the western half
- bounded on the southwest by Niagara Falls
- retention time is 6 years

Ontario Lakes and Waterways

N
W—E
S

0   100   200   300 Km

Great Lakes

The important thing about Lake _____

is that it is_____

It is _____

it _____

it _____

But the important thing about Lake _____

_____

_____

_____

_____

_____

_____

_____

Lake Superior

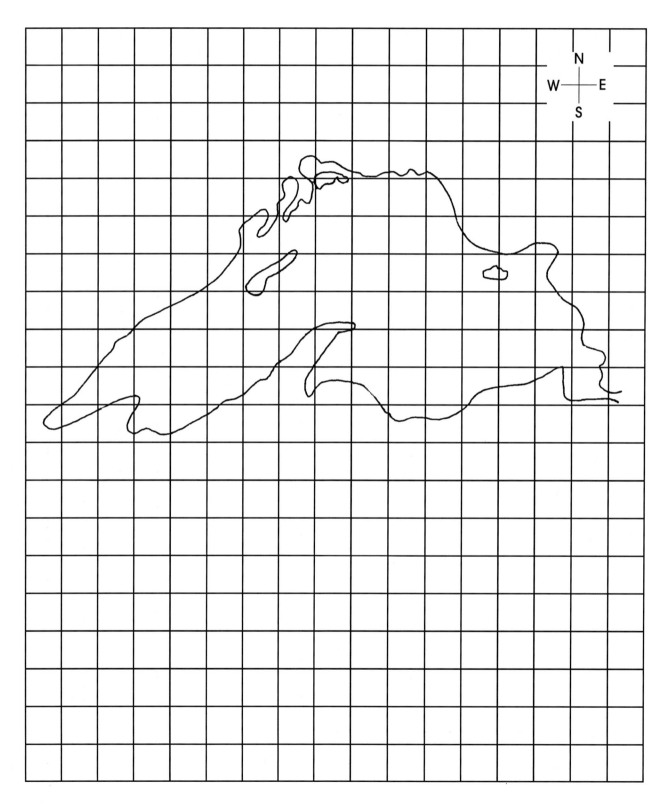

Lake Michigan

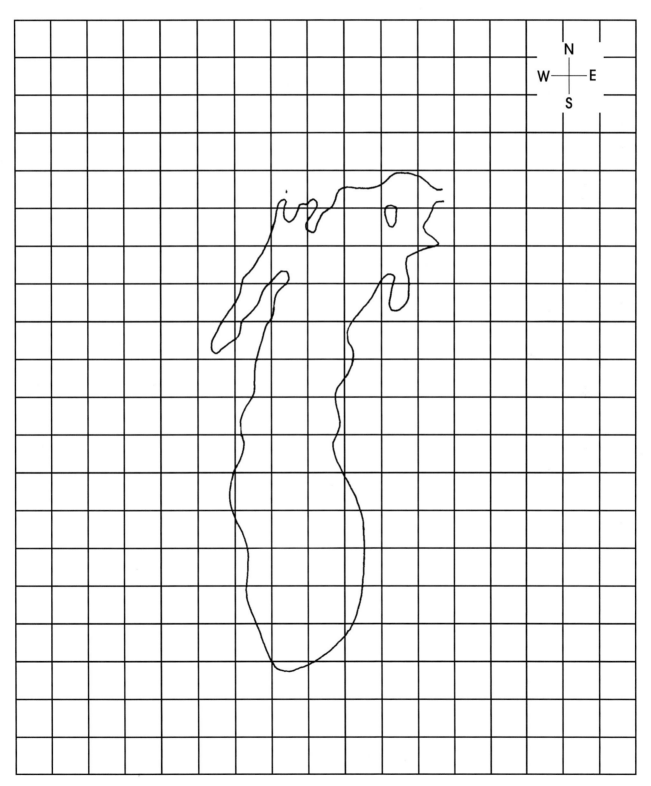

Lake Huron

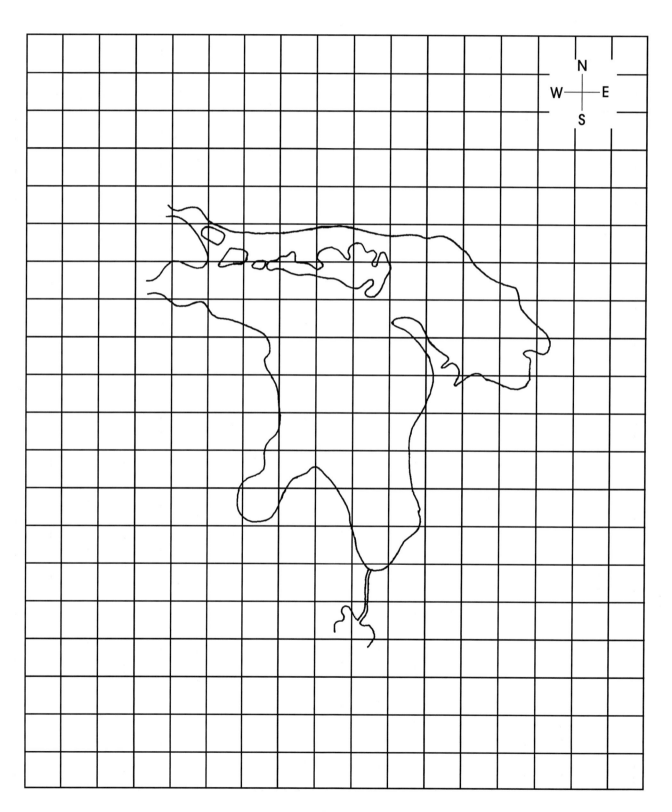

Lake Erie

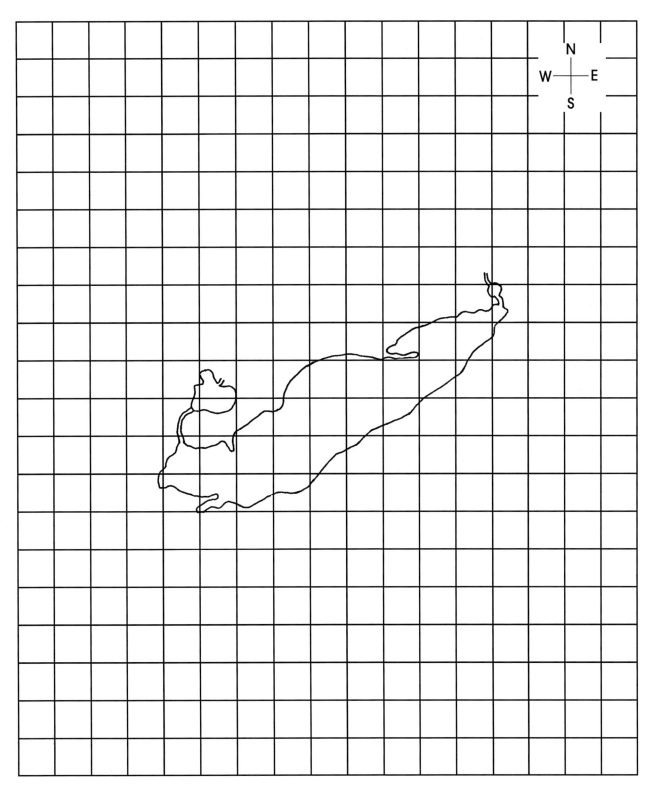

Lake Ontario

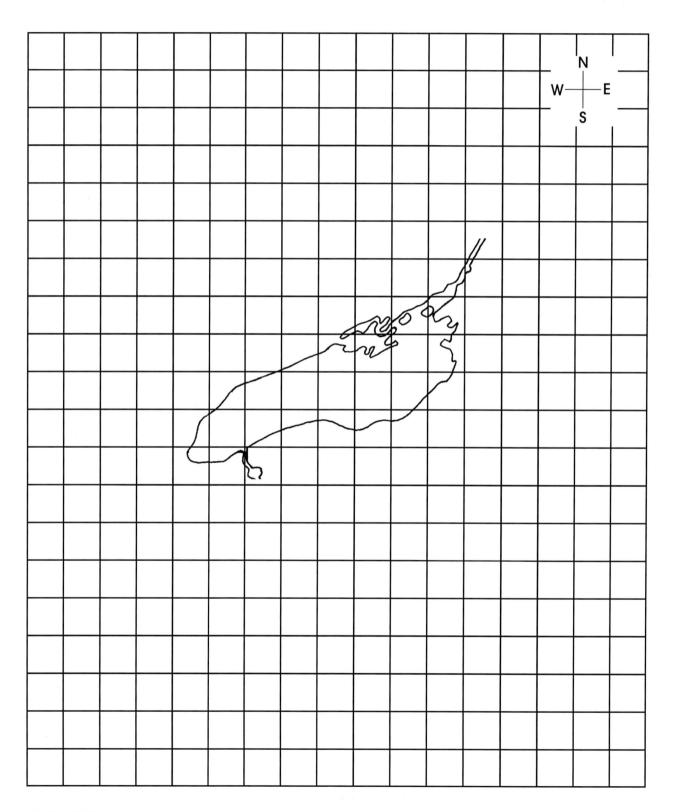

10 A River System

Background Information for Teachers

Ontario contains over one-quarter of the world's supply of fresh water. The lakes and rivers were important to the early settlement of the province. They were the first highways, moving goods and people throughout the province. As industry developed, the water has been used to produce hydroelectricity. The Great Lakes and the St. Lawrence River allow goods from all over the world to be moved far inland.

As ships increased in size, the waterways underwent human-made changes in order to circumvent narrow, shallow, or rapid water. The first canal was built in 1825 around the Lachine Rapids. In the 1950s, the governments of Canada and the United States built the St. Lawrence Seaway. Locks were constructed, lakes and rivers were deepened, and three huge dams were built. The St. Lawrence Seaway allows ships to be raised over 183 metres between the Atlantic Ocean and Lake Superior.

River Terms and Definitions

Mouth: where the river meets the ocean or lake
Source: the place where a river starts
Tributary: a river that runs into another, larger river
Branch: an extension of a river
Delta: the area around the mouth of the river created by soil deposits
Flow: the speed of the water

Materials

- materials for making land/lake/river models (clay, cake pans, soil, sand, small stones, twigs, jar lids)
- containers of water
- sponges
- chart paper
- markers
- toothpicks
- construction paper
- scissors
- wall map of Canada
- map of Canada showing population density
- reference material on the St. Lawrence Seaway
- lined paper for a learning response

Activity: Part One

As a class, review the students' understanding of lakes from the previous lesson. Ask:

- What is a lake?
- What surrounds the water in a lake?
- What is below the water in a lake?
- Where does the water in a lake come from?

Explain to students that they are going to make a model of a section of land and a lake. Form working groups of students and provide each group with a pan, clay, jar lid, soil, sand, stones, and twigs. Have the students build a section of land inside the pan with clay. Models should include an elevated section with the jar lid recessed into it. The jar lid will represent a lake. Fill the lid almost full with water. Cover the land section with a thin layer of soil and sand. Sprinkle the land model with small stones and twigs. Once the models are completed, ask:

- What do the parts of the models represent in the real landscape?

▶

- Where would rain collect if it fell on this area?
- What happens to the water in the lake when it gets too full?

Provide the students with water and sponges. Have students soak the sponges in water, then squeeze them to create "rain" over the lake. Encourage them to observe where the water goes when the lake overflows. Ask:

- What would you call this stream of water that is flowing downhill? (river)
- What happens to the soil and sand as the water runs over it?
- Where will it go?

Print the following words on chart paper: *river, source, delta, tributary, branch,* and *mouth.* Discuss each term and allow students an opportunity to give their own ideas as to what each word means. Provide students with a definition of each word, using the Background Information for Teachers.

Have students locate each term on their model. Make a small flag with construction paper and toothpicks and post the word on the model (branches and tributaries may have to be manipulated on some models).

Have students draw diagrams of their river model on activity sheet A and write a description to go with each model, using the terms included on the sheet.

Activity Sheet A

Directions to students:

Draw a diagram of your model, then use the words in the box to write a descriptive paragraph (2.10.1).

Activity: Part Two

Display a map of Canada. Have the students locate the St. Lawrence River and trace its path from the ocean to the Great Lakes. Ask:

- What would the river be used for?
- If the river and lakes were not there, how would transportation be more difficult?

Now display a map of Canada showing population density. Review the legend. Ask:

- Where do most people live in Canada?
- Why is the area around the St. Lawrence River so heavily populated? (e.g., recreation, drinking water, transportation)
- What do you think would happen if the river was too narrow or shallow for ships to travel on?
- Have you ever floated a paper boat or a toothpick through a puddle system?
- What sometimes stops the boat from moving? (obstacles, shallow water)

Note: If weather permits, this is a good outdoor activity to show students how barriers can inhibit a vessel's movement.

Explain that the same thing can happen in large bodies of water. Sometimes lakes and rivers can be too shallow or narrow, or have obstacles blocking waterways. Humans can change lakes and rivers to help ships and the goods that they carry move through the water. The St. Lawrence River and the Great Lakes have been changed so that goods can move from Montreal to Lake Superior. This system is called the St. Lawrence Seaway. Ask:

- Do you think that these changes affected the environment?
- Why would the seaway be important to Ontario and to Canada?

10

Provide students with activity sheet B (2.10.2), as well as a variety of reference materials on the St. Lawrence Seaway. Have them conduct research in order to complete the activity sheet.

Activity Sheet B

Directions to students:

Use the activity sheet to record information about the St. Lawrence Seaway (2.10.2).

Extension

Visit a local river or stream. Have students sketch the river and the surrounding land. If possible, adopt a river. Visit it during the different seasons. Sketch and photograph it at different times of the year. Present a picture essay at the end of the year.

Note: Follow water safety precautions at all times when around water. Ensure that these safety rules are reviewed with students prior to visits to the river.

Activity Centre

Place outline maps of Canada, atlases, and small cards labelled with Canadian rivers and lakes at the centre. Challenge students to locate the rivers and lakes using the map skills that they have learned. Label the maps.

Assessment Suggestion

Have students complete the student self-assessment sheet on page 19 to reflect on their learning about river systems.

A River System

Draw a diagram of your model:

lake	delta	mouth
river	tributary	water
source	branch	

Use these words to describe your model: _____

_____

_____

_____

_____

_____

The St. Lawrence Seaway

Diagram of the St. Lawrence Seaway:

Five things I learned about the St. Lawrence Seaway:

_____

_____

_____

_____

_____

The St. Lawrence Seaway is important because:

_____

_____

_____

11 | Ontario's Resources and Industry

Background Information for Teachers

Ontario is Canada's main producer of nickel, cobalt, salt, and magnesium. The Canadian Shield also has zinc, platinum, uranium, oil, natural gas, copper, gold, silver, and iron ore. Ontario's pulp and paper industry is the second largest in Canada. The area called the Golden Horseshoe, from Oshawa to St. Catharines, has many factories, businesses, and banking institutions. The auto industry has many large plants in this area. Ontario's farmland is used for livestock, fruits, and vegetables.

Materials

- municipal maps with grid systems (any city map includes this as a means of finding locations)
- blank grid (included. Make an overhead transparency of this sheet.) (2.11.1)
- overhead projector
- nonpermanent overhead pens
- sheet titled, "Ontario's Natural Resources and Industry" (included. Make an overhead transparency of this sheet.) (2.11.2)
- books or clipboards to use as barriers between the partners
- pencils

Activity

Ask students if any of them have ever played the game Battleship. If any have, let them give an oral explanation of the game. Explain to students that Battleship works on a grid system. Grid systems are used to find locations on maps as well.

Distribute examples of grid systems on municipal maps. Discuss how the grid system is used to find street locations on the map.

Display the blank grid sheet on the overhead (2.11.1). Using an overhead pen, mark an X on the grid at the B3 location. Ask:

- How can I describe the location of the X?
- Who can mark an X at C5?

Repeat with several more examples until you are confident that students understand the grid system.

Now display the sheet titled, "Ontario's Natural Resources and Industry" (2.11.2) on the overhead. Cover the right-hand side of the sheet so that only the pictures and title are visible. Remind the students that natural resources are things in the environment that we can use and sell. Industry is the production or manufacturing of an item in some form of factory. The selling and buying of natural resources and products from industry create Ontario's economy.

Ask students to predict what each pictorial symbol represents. Uncover the words as students predict. Divide the class into pairs of students and provide one partner with activity sheet A (2.11.3) and one with activity sheet B (2.11.4). Each sheet shows a map of Ontario with only some of its natural resources and industries labelled. Stress to students that they are not allowed to look at each other's maps. Students can sit together with a book or barrier between them. They will take turns giving grid clues so that their partner can locate and draw the missing symbols on his or her map. When they think they are finished, they can remove the barrier and compare maps for accuracy. Discuss the completed maps. Ask:

- What natural resources are found in each land region?
- Why do you think most manufacturing is found around the St. Lawrence River?
- What do you remember about the Canadian Shield?

11

- Why are mines found in the Canadian Shield?
- What land region is most farming found in? Why?
- Why are there not many farming symbols found in the Canadian Shield?

Activity Sheets A and B

Directions to students:

Work with your partner to complete your map, using grid clues to locate natural resources and industry in Ontario (2.11.3, 2.11.4).

Extensions

- Visit a place of business in your community that is involved in the production of one of Ontario's major resources or industries. Conduct an interview with an employee of the business. Write a report on the processes involved in producing the item.

- Research the travels of an item produced in Ontario. Where, in the world, does it go? How does it get there?

Activity Centre

Place examples of Ontario's natural resources and industries in a centre (water, car parts, rocks, minerals, vegetables). Have students identify what the item is and where it comes from in the province. Have students draw a sketch map of Ontario and locate the items on the map.

Blank Grid

6					
5					
4					
3					
2					
1					

A   B   C   D   E   F

Ontario's Natural Resources and Industry

 vegetables

 cars

 gold

 pulp and paper

 chemicals

 forestry

 steel

 nickel

fruit

Ontario Resources and Industry I

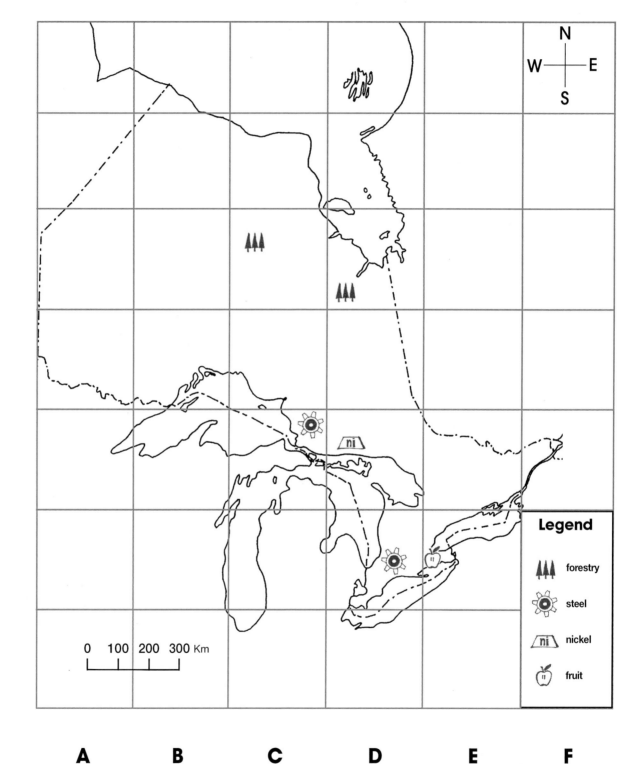

Ontario Resources and Industry II

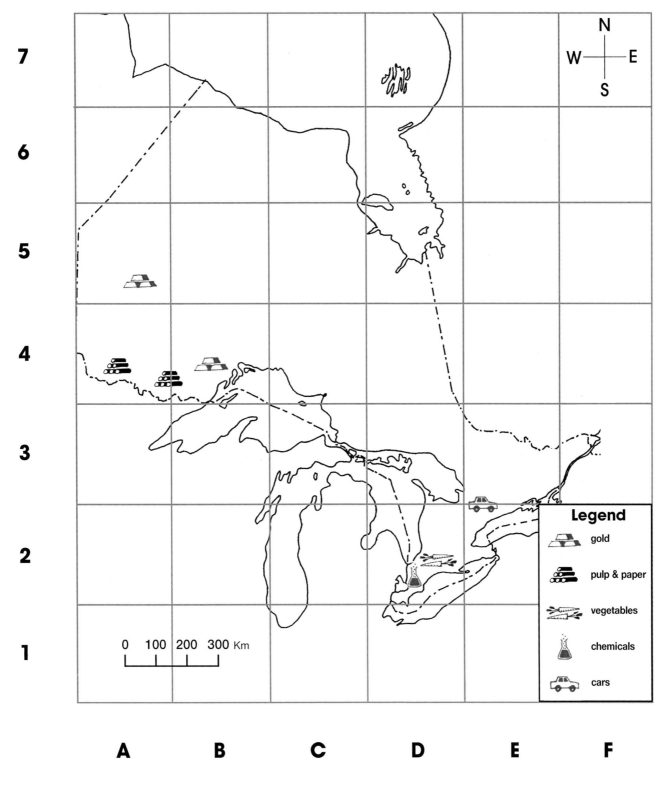

Legend

gold

pulp & paper

vegetables

chemicals

cars

0 100 200 300 Km

12 Ontario's Communities

Materials

- landscape pictures of Ontario's land regions (used in lesson 8)
- student maps of Ontario's natural resources and industry (from lesson 11)
- chart paper
- markers
- tourist information on Ontario's communities (the local tourism office is a good source for brochures, posters, and magazines)
- bookmarked web sites on Ontario tourism and communities
- bookmarked web sites of rail, bus, plane routes, fares, and schedules
- Ontario road maps
- pencil crayons
- graph paper (2.12.3)

Activity: Part One

Display the landscape pictures and, as a class, sort the pictures based on the land region in Ontario.

Provide students with copies of activity sheets A and B (2.12.1, 2.12.2). Review Ontario's natural resources and industries presented in the previous lesson, referring to the students' maps. Have students read each community introduction on activity sheet A, and select a community in Ontario where these people could come from. Have students choose a symbol to represent the community (e.g., a coloured dot), and record this symbol on activity sheet A. Now have the students record the symbol on the map and in the legend on activity sheet B.

Discuss the students' predictions and record on chart paper a list of possible communities that each person could live in.

Discuss with students that communities exist based on the economic opportunities in the region. Manufacturing provides huge numbers of jobs. Therefore, the communities that exist around manufacturing plants have large populations. Fishing and hunting communities have smaller populations and exist where a large amount of wildlife maintain their natural habitat. Mining towns have built up around found deposits of particular minerals. If the economic reason for the community changes, the community itself often changes. For example, if a mine closes down, people may move away, and the community's population and businesses will decrease.

At the bottom of activity sheet A, have the students write a community introduction based on a community of their choice. Have them choose a symbol for this community and place it on the map and legend on activity sheet B.

Have students share their introductions while their classmates attempt to identify possible communities that are being referred to.

Activity Sheets A and B

Directions to students:

Read each community introduction. Use the information you have about land regions, natural resources, and industries in Ontario to identify a community that this person could live in. Choose a symbol for each community. Record the symbol below the community introduction and on the map and legend on activity sheet B (2.12.1, 2.12.2).

Activity: Part Two

Begin the lesson by discussing transportation. Ask:

- How did you get to school today?

Discuss why students made certain transportation choices. For example:

12

Bus: live a farther distance from school

Car: parents drive, weather was cold and rainy

Walk: good exercise, close distance to school

Brainstorm a list of all the possible ways to travel. As the list is generated, discuss the positives and negatives of each type of transportation. Explain to students that they are going to plan an imaginary field trip in Ontario.

Note: You may want to refer to The Magic School Bus series as examples of imaginary class field trips.

Divide the class into working groups. Provide each group with tourist material and activity sheet C. Also introduce students to bookmarked web sites that may help them plan their field trips. Have students review the tourist information and select a place that they would like to visit in Ontario. Review the expectations for the completion of this task, and record them on chart paper:

1. Transportation information: Plan the transportation to this location. Use information from maps, transportation schedules, and fare schedules to complete the sheet.

2. Draw a sketch map of Ontario. Mark your own community and destination. Draw the route that you will take on your field trip.

3. Tourist brochure: Use tourist information to complete the tourist brochure about the community you are visiting. It should include:

- illustrated cover with the name of the community
- where the community is located
- how to get to the community
- things to see and do
- places to stay

4. Journal entry: Pretend you have gone on the field trip. Make an illustration and write a journal entry about your experience.

Provide plenty of class time for the completion of this project. When completed, have the groups share their field-trip itinerary with their classmates.

Activity Sheet C

Note: This is a four-page activity sheet.

Directions to students:

Use the activity sheets to plan and write about an imaginary field trip to an Ontario community (2.12.3).

Extension

Plan and go on an actual field trip to a place of interest in your own community or a nearby neighbouring community.

Assessment Suggestion

As a class, develop criteria for the field-trip itinerary presentations. These may include:

- accurate transportation information
- detailed map
- creative journal entry
- clear speaking voices

List these criteria on the rubric on page 16 and record results during presentations.

Date:_____   Name:_____

Ontario Community Introduction

Read each introduction. Decide where in Ontario each of these Canadians might live. There are many possibilities. Support your answer with facts. Choose a symbol for each community. Place the symbol on the map and legend.

Hi, my name is Joseph McKay. My family owns a hunting and fishing lodge.

This person might live in _____

Symbol:

Hi, my name is Emily Tourand. We live in a large city. My parents work in an automobile factory.

This person might live in _____

Symbol:

Hi, My name is Connor Seddon. I live in a small town. My parents and many of my friends' parents work at the mine.

This person might live in _____

Symbol:

Hi, my name is Maclean Boyd. Did you know that some of the vegetables you ate for dinner last night may have come from my family's farm?

This person might live in _____

Symbol:

Hi, my name is Keely Lyons. My mother works for a large international bank in our city. My father teaches at the university.

This person might live in _____

Symbol:

Hi, my name is _____

_____

_____

This person might live in _____

Symbol:

Ontario Communities

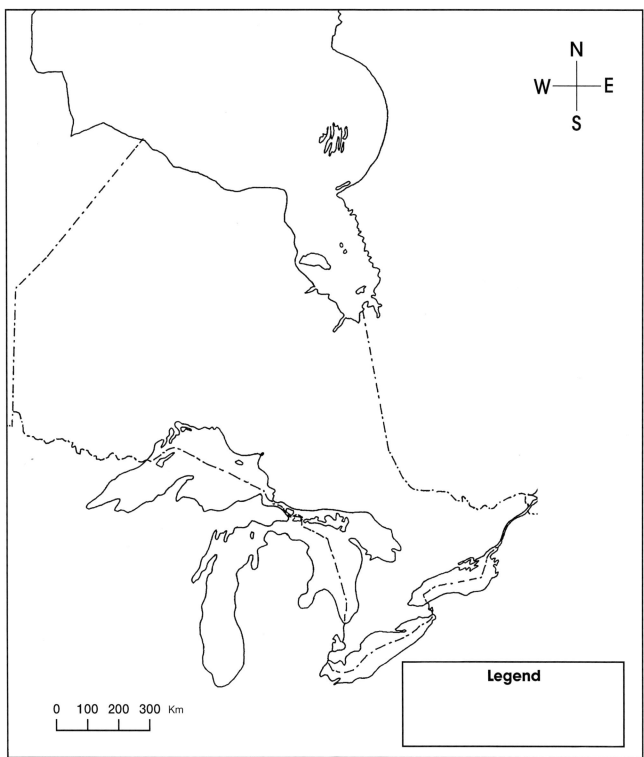

N
W—E
S

0 100 200 300 Km

Legend

Date:_____   Name: _____

_____

_____

_____

Field Trip

Ticket to _____

Travelling by _____

Departing _____

Arriving _____

Cost _____

We chose this form of transportation because:

_____

_____

_____

_____

_____

_____

_____

_____

Map of Our Fantasy Field Trip to _____

-- Fold --

Things to see and do in

-- Fold --

Journal Entry of Our Fantasy Field Trip to

_____

_____
_____
_____
_____
_____
_____
_____
_____
_____

13 | The Environment and the Economy

Background Information for Teachers

The economy is closely tied to the enviroment of any region. Many economic developments have detrimental effects to the environment; for example, over-fishing on the Grand Banks, logging in the forests of British Columbia, pit mining in the Canadian Shield, and air pollution and acid rain from manufacturing.

Materials

- chart paper
- markers
- resource materials related to environmental issues, including nonfiction books, CDs, bookmarked web sites

Activity

Print the word *environment* on chart paper. Brainstorm with students any environmental issues that they are aware of. Add other environmental issues to the list. These may include:

- air pollution
- water pollution
- land pollution
- global warming
- greenhouse effect
- landfills
- logging/deforestation
- fuel emissions
- over-fishing

Choose one of the issues, such as air pollution. Create a web that identifies the causes of the problem, as well as possible solutions.

Provide students with copies of the activity sheet. Assign each student one of the environmental issues to research. (More than one student can work on the same topic.

Students may also select an environmental issue not listed.) Provide research materials so students gain some background knowledge and gather information on the environmental issue.

Note: At this level, the complex details of environmental issues may be difficult for students to comprehend. Approach the issue based on the students' experiences and understanding. For example: Logging: Logging is necessary for products such as paper and furniture. Trees are important to the environment because they produce oxygen and provide wildlife habitats.

Note: If students come across the more political issues during this lesson, they can be dealt with based on the students' interests and abilities. The main focus of this lesson is to create awareness that economic growth affects the environment, and that people need to be aware of and work toward solutions.

Guide the students through the completion of the activity sheet. Have the students complete the first page of the activity sheet based on their research and their own opinions. On the second page, have them create a question to ask people about this environmental issue. As homework, have students ask their family or neighbours the question that they created.

Note: Explain that opinions are different from facts, but that people's opinions may help them to understand the different points of view involved in these issues.

Have students write a paragraph that would help make people aware of this environmental issue.

Encourage students to share their findings with the class in order to further understand the relationship between economic growth and the environment.

13

Activity Sheet

Note: This is a two-page activity sheet.

Directions to students:

Use the activity sheet to identify the issue, gather information, and write a paragraph that makes others aware of the issue (2.13.1).

Extensions

- Challenge students to write letters or become active in finding solutions for environmental issues.

- Brainstorm with students ways that they can make a difference (e.g., recycling paper, conserving water and energy).

- Research ways that environmental issues positively affect the economy, such as recycling programs and tree planting.

The Environment and the Economy

My Environmental Issue: _____

_____

1. I would describe my issue as: _____

_____

_____

_____

_____

2. In my opinion, some ways to solve problems related to

this issue are: _____

_____

_____

_____

_____

_____

_____

_____

3. If I could ask other people one question about this issue, it would be: _____

_____

Who I Asked	Opinion

4. To help make people more aware of the issue, this is what I would tell them: _____

_____

_____

_____

_____

_____

14 | Culminating Activities

Materials

- photocopy paper
- access to a photocopier
- pencils
- pencil crayons
- scissors
- map of Canada
- map of Ontario
- plain paper
- baseball caps or canvas painter hats
- fabric paints
- paintbrushes
- shoeboxes
- atlases
- rulers
- camera

Note: The following activities are ways to bring closure to this unit on Canada's provinces and territories.

Activity One: Postcard Journey

This activity can be done for Ontario or for Canada. Give each student a blank piece of photocopy paper. Have the students draw a 10 cm line somewhere on the paper and write their name in a corner of the sheet. Collect the papers and place them in the paper tray of the photocopier. Photocopy an outline map of Canada or Ontario onto each of the sheets. This will produce an outline map with a route on it. When students receive their paper back, they can research an imaginary journey along this route. Have the students draw four or five postcards from different locations on their journey, then on the back of the postcards record information on the weather and activities they might have done while visiting this place.

Activity Two: Alphabet Books

Have students develop alphabet books about Canada or Ontario. The books can include writing and illustrations. For example:

A is for Alberta, a province rich in oil.
B is for Brandon, a city in western Manitoba.
C is for Cape Breton, in Canada's Maritimes.

Activity Three: Wearing My Canadian Hat

Obtain inexpensive baseball caps and fabric paints for this activity (paint stores will often donate canvas painting caps). Have students reflect on what they have learned about Canada. Using symbols, have them design a hat that is truly Canadian. The symbols should include Canada's place in the world, resources, animals, weather, and climate. Have the students design the rough draft on paper first, then use fabric paint to complete their hats. Take pictures of each student wearing his or her hat. Have them complete a written explanation of what their symbols mean.

Activity Four: The Canadian Box

Each student will need a cardboard box with a removable lid (shoebox). Have the students use a grid to copy a map of Canada from an atlas. They can then colour and label the map (provinces, capital cities, own city, Ottawa) and glue the map on the top lid of the box. Now have students decorate the four outside panels of the box with the following:

- the Canadian flag
- a landscape collage
- symbols and pictures depicting Canada's economy
- symbols and pictures depicting Canada's culture.

The inside of the box can be used in the following ways:

- to hold an important Canadian artifact or souvenirs
- to create a Canadian diorama
- to hold trivia questions and answers about Canada